Gi

Costa

Dénia – Calp – Benidorm – Alcoi – Alicante – Orihuela

51 selected walks on the coast and in the mountains

ROTHER • MUNICH

ROTHER Walking Guides

Foreword

The 'white coast' has a lot more to offer than a simple beach holiday – not only the spectacular mountains and gorges, but also the marvellous spring blossom and warm autumn days have attracted walkers and climbers from all over Europe for decades. High barren mountains with deeply furrowed ridges providing shelter against cold northerly winds are a contrast to the coast with its fertile garden landscapes and widespread fruit plantations.

Since the largest mountain regions are situated close to the northern tourist resorts, this is where most of the walks in this guide are located. However, walks in some of the more remote *sierras* in the province of Alicante (in Valencian Alacant) are also described. They range from short easy paths up to beautiful viewpoints to challenging ascents of some iconic mountains and dominant landmarks in the area. There are ridge walks on solitary high mountains, descents into deep rocky gorges, plus a walk round a neglected island gem. Many walks lead along forest tracks, while others follow ancient mule paths or even hunters' paths. This guide also offers some beautiful and, in part, easier versions of established classic walks. Although you will not usually find yourself walking very far from a village, you will meet few other walkers along the way. The characteristic features of the Costa Blanca countryside are primarily the terraces with their skilfully constructed dry stone walls that run across every hillside, in every valley, even up to some high and improbable places. You will discover valleys full of almond and olive trees, springs, caves and the ruins of ancient Moorish castles. The Romans, and then particularly the Moors, left their influence on this landscape with their irrigation systems.

The walks selected for this book try to accommodate all levels of ability, including some walks that are suitable for the whole family. Changes can often occur due to new fencing, road construction, housing developments and, of course, the constant effects of nature. In preparation for this second edition we have come across several noticeable signs of change, such as the wash-out on paths due to unusually heavy rainfall and an increased incidence of forest fires, both of which can modify the line of the route, although it must be said that the signage has much improved. Please notify the publishers if you come across any other changes to these route descriptions.

I would like to thank the following walking companions for helping me check the second edition – Pat Swales, Pam and Terry Lee, Christopher North, Pat Grey, Terry Gifford and lastly Martin Harrison-Smith whose enthusiastic help with recording the GPS routes was invaluable. Thanks also go to Cordula Rabe for her encouragement and knowledgeable help in editing this book.

I hope you enjoy many varied and exciting adventures on these walks in the Costa Blanca.

Sella, summer 2013   Gill Round

Contents

General tips

Use of the guide

Each of the walks starts with a short characterisation and is followed by an informative fact-file section and a detailed description of the route. A small walking map showing the line of the route and waypoints (see GPS tracks on p. 10), as well as the height profile, give the walker a first impression. A glossary at the back of the book provides the most common words in Valencian and Castilian that might be useful to the mountain walker and in the index you will find all the relevant names of mountains, starting points, locations and landmarks. The overview maps show the location of each walk.

Grade

Most of the walks run along clear paths, often along yellow and white marked PR-CV or red and white marked GR paths (see below) and are therefore recommended for less experienced walkers too. A good level of fitness and sure-footedness are required sometimes when there is a considerable height difference to overcome. Sturdy footwear is essential in all cases.

In order to assess the grade more efficiently the walk numbers are given in three different colours as follows:

Easy These paths are mostly wide, may be steep over short sections, or moderately steep overall. There are generally no problems with route finding and they are undertaken quite safely in poor weather conditions.

Moderate Moderate walks are strenuous in places, due to their steeper inclines or length, and make more demands on stamina and fitness. Sure-footedness is essential and also some previous experience of walking in the mountains.

Difficult These difficult walks are often poorly waymarked, run frequently over rough ground and sometimes may be very long. The height differences on these walks are much greater and only experienced, surefooted and fit mountain walkers with a good sense of direction should undertake them.

Easier alternatives to red and black numbered walks are referred to wherever possible in the fact-file section.

Access

The relatively well developed bus network connects the coastal resorts, but unfortunately does not reach most of the starting points inland. If there is a bus service to a particular village at all, the bus leaves very early in the morning and often doesn't return until 18.00 at the earliest. Bearing in mind the inadequate public transport, the walks in this book have been devised mainly as circular walks where the starting and end points are identical. Therefore, renting a car is recommended. There is a big choice of cars for rent in larger towns and at the airport, but it is advisable to book a hire car in advance of your travel and pick it up at the airport. Driving in Spain is fairly straightforward, but be careful along winding roads inland – there's a tendency for Spanish drivers to drive in the middle of the road!

Taxi ranks can be found in larger towns, usually near to the train station, but journeys by taxi are often expensive.

Equipment

Sturdy footwear with good soles is essential for every walk. Most walks require the usual walking gear – comfortable and practical clothing, protection against all weather conditions, sun cream and a hat. You will rarely be able to buy food along the way and springs may have dried up, so be sure to take enough provisions with you and in particular plenty of water, at least a litre for each person. Walking poles are definitely recommended, especially for descents down steep or loose scree paths.

Best season

Climate change is affecting Spain, as it is everywhere, and the weather is not as predictable as before. However, generally speaking, you can still go walking almost all year round on the Costa Blanca. The best weather can be found in spring (March to May) when most of the flowers are in bloom; the almond blossom in early February is also an impressive sight. You might have to contend with a *gota fría* in late September (heavy rainfall with the

Symbole

🚌	accesible by bus	∴	archaeologic site
❌	places to eat on the way	▲	viewing tower
👪	suitable for children	🔆	lighthouse
⬤▲	village, town with bar/restaurant	⌐ ⌐	turn-off left / right
⬤	staffed hut/restaurant on the way	∩	cave
⬜	mountain hut, shelter	⋏	campsite
P	car park	开	picnic site
†)(	summit / pass, col	✲	viewpoint
⸸	church, chapel	◉	spring
▲	castle, ruin	▨	swimming

9

danger of flooding), otherwise autumn is a good season for walking; even in winter walking conditions are normally excellent although some days snowfall might occur in higher regions. Summer, on the other hand, is usually far too hot for the majority of walks described in this guide – the heat, particularly on long walks, or those without any shade, should not be underestimated and it is therefore absolutely essential that you take lots of water with you on every walk during warmer seasons.

It is worth noting that sunny weather on the coast does not necessarily mean that the sun is also shining inland or in the mountains, and you should always be prepared for a change in the weather and pack the necessary gear. Sudden mist or clouds may appear in the high mountains in the afternoon, but are unlikely to mean rain. Thunderstorms are unusual in summer, but not unknown.

Dangers

Most of the walks described in this guide run along good, clear paths, but one or two of the more difficult mountain walks lead across rough ground with poor paths. Problematic places, e.g. scree traverses or sections of scrambling, are given special mention in the text. Do not underestimate the dangers of loose stones underfoot!

Dogs can be a problem in remote farmsteads. Most of them are tied up, but you should nevertheless keep a respectful distance; if you should come across a dog on the loose, bending down as if to pick up a stone is usually sufficient to send it scampering away.

The pine processionary is a plain, night-active moth. Its caterpillars live in web-spun nests from January to April on pine trees which they often strip of their needles, and when they leave their nest they travel nose to tail in a line

GPS tracks

The GPS data for this guide is available in a free download from the Rother website (www.rother.de) for which you will need the following password: wfCoBgb02782pA (username: gast).

All the GPS routes were recorded on the ground by the author and coordinated with the digital maps of the National Institute of Geography (IGN). The tracks and the waypoints have been checked by the author and the publishers to the best of their knowledge. Nevertheless mistakes and variations cannot be ruled out. It is also possible that some details might have changed in the meantime. GPS data is, without doubt, an excellent planning and navigational tool, but careful preparation, good route-finding ability as well as experience in judging the conditions on the day are essential. One should never totally rely on the GPS device and its data for following a route.

The Top 10 walks on the Costa Blanca

Vall de Laguar

Along a beautiful ancient stepped path down into the deeply cut gorge of the Río Girona. Part of the walk runs along the popular route known as the Barranc d'Infern (Walk 2, 4 hrs.).

Els Arcs

Peaceful and interesting walk to two spectacular rock arches that, over millions of years, have been carved out of the limestone (Walk 8, 2¼ hrs.).

Penya El Castellet

Walk with fabulous views along the ridge of the Sierra de Serrella above the Guadalest valley and an ascent to an impressively situated castle ruin (Walk 10, 2½ hrs.).

Circuit of the Sierra de Bèrnia

This popular walk leads past the site of an old fortress onto the north side of the mountain range, then returns through the *forat*, a natural tunnel through the rock, with marvellous views across the bay of Altea (Walk 13, 3¾ hrs.).

Peñón de Ifach

A classic route on the Costa Blanca: a short, but exciting ascent onto a dominant landmark on the Costa Blanca (Walk 16, 2 hrs.).

Puig Campana

Ascent of the legendary Puig Campana, the 1408m high mountain giant, visible from a long way off with its striking notch. This is a classic walk on the Costa Blanca and two alternatives are offered for the ascent onto this spectacular mountain (Walk 22, 6¾ hrs.).

Monte Ponoig

Walk through a fascinating countryside onto the 'sleeping lion' and descent via the highwaymen's pass (Walk 23, 4 hrs.).

Peña de Sella

Walk onto the Alto de la Peña de Sella, a long mountain range behind the idyllically situated village of Sella, with a wide panorama high above the Barranc de l'Arc (Walk 26, 2¼ hrs.).

Sierra de Aitana

Interesting walk onto the highest mountain in the province of Alicante with unique views both of the coast and far (Walk 28, 4 hrs.).

Pas de Goleró

Short round walk through dramatic mountain scenery characterised by terraces and pine forests, with a descent of an impressive narrow and steep pass (Walk 32, 2¼ hrs.).

across the ground. Their tiny hairs cause itching, a rash or even asthma. If you should inadvertently come into contact with them it's advisable for you to take a shower as soon as possible and wash all your clothes. The caterpillars are especially dangerous for dogs and can even be life-threatening. Consequently, direct contact with them must be avoided at all costs.

Walking times

The times given are the actual walking times, at an average tempo and do not include stops. From experience, the times can be increased by up to another 50 percent and depend on the walker's fitness and prevailing weather conditions, and in some cases, the possible deterioration of the path.

The network of paths on the Costa Blanca is large and in most cases well marked.

Maps

The basis of the maps in this guide is that of the 1:50,000 map of the *Cartografía Militar de España* (with Castilian place names) and the *Instituto Geográfico Nacional* (IGN, 1:25 000, with Valencian place names; sales and distribution: *Centro Nacional de Información Geográfica*, CNIG, www.cnig.es). The spelling of place names etc. in the route descriptions is the one most commonly used in that area although the names on the signposts are mostly in Valencian. Often the Spanish and Valencian names are quite similar; where there might be some confusion, the alternative name has been added in brackets (eg. Torremanzanas is in Valencian, La Torre de les Maçanes). Each walk refers to the map/maps to a scale of 1:25 000 (IGN-CNIG) for that particular walking area. Maps for the Marina Alta and Marina Baixa by Terra Firma are available locally as well as two hiking maps published by El Tossal Cartografies for La Serrella and La Serra de Mariola. All are available before you travel from www.stanfords.co.uk or www.themapshop.co.uk, or when you arrive from Librería Europa, Calle Oscar Esplá 2 in Calp (www.libreria-europa-calpe.com) where you can also obtain flower and bird guides; the owner is English and speaks several languages. Alternatively maps can be ordered from La Tienda Verde (www.latiendaverde.com) in Spain. Tourist offices can also be a good source of regional maps and walking leaflets.

PR-CV and GR walking paths on the Costa Blanca

Many of the walks in the region's comprehensive network of paths are marked as PR-CVs (Pequeño Recorrido de la Comunidad Valenciana, yellow and white) and Walk 40 in this guide follows sections of the red and white marked GR 7 long distance path (Gran Recorrido). There are also local SL-CV hiking paths (Senda Local de la Comunidad Valenciana, green and white). The waymarkers, two parallel lines of colour, can be explained as follows: '=/X' denotes correct/incorrect route, 'll', uphill, '«', change in direction. Information about all three of these types of paths can be found on the internet under www.cma.gva.es, link: Medio Natural – Senda Verde – Red de Senderos. The walks in this guide sometimes run along parts of a PR-CV marked path or even follow the whole route, but often combine new paths with previously waymarked routes. Some walks are waymarked with cairns – please rebuild any cairns that have fallen down. Many of the paths are newly or freshly waymarked each year.

Accommodation, places to eat and gastronomy

Booking a package holiday is the most practical way of finding accommodation, but there is a wide selection of hotels, *hostales* (cheap bed and breakfast) and apartments on the coast. Good priced accommodation is also offered in remoter areas in *casas rurales* (sometimes self-catering accommodation, sometimes with breakfast and lunch and/or dinner).

Tips about campsites and *refugios* (basic mountain huts), where available, can be found in the fact-file section and is also obtainable on the internet under www.costablanca.org, www.comunitatvalenciana.com and www.campings.net.

There are bars in almost all of the villages where you can eat simply and cheaply. Most bars and restaurants offer a selection of *tapas* (small snacks); small fish (*pescaditos*), prawns (*gambas*) and baby squid (*calamares*) are very popular. Also particularly worth trying are the delicious local rice dishes, e.g. Valencian paella, a rice dish with rabbit, chicken, red pepper and chick peas, amongst other things. There are also seafood paellas (*paella de marisco*) or an Alicante version with both meat and fish (*paella mixta*). Restaurants are usually closed on Mondays and tend to be very busy at the weekend.

A baguette-type loaf (*barra de pan*), *coca* (pizza-like base topped with either sausage, mushroom, artichoke, black pudding and/or tomato paste) and *empanada* (pasty filled with tuna and tomato or spinach) are some of the regional snacks which can be bought from the baker's (*horno*, Valencian *forn*; open every day except Christmas day).

Throughout the region you will come across beautiful picnic areas (*áreas recreativas*) that are equipped with tables, benches, often barbecues and toilets as well. They are particularly busy at weekends when the Spanish like to make a family trip into the countryside. Due to the danger of forest fires, the use of the barbecues and open camp fires is usually forbidden in the summer months.

A stroll through the weekly market – here in Sella – is a must for every holidaymaker on the Costa Blanca.

Walking in the Costa Blanca

The community of Valencia, one of 17 autonomous regions in Spain, consists of 3 provinces – Castellón, Valencia and Alicante. Alicante's coastline, known as the Costa Blanca, stretches over 200km and the province is divided into 9 *comarcas* (local districts). On the coast, wonderful long sandy beaches alternate with small remote bays and sheer cliffs, but the Alicante region stretches far inland where mountains rise more than 1000m.

Good starting points for walks are, for example, Dénia and Xàbia (Walks 1–6), Calp (Walks 7–17) and Altea (Walks 18–21) on the coast and Sella inland (Walks 22–33).

Geology

About 100 million years ago this area of Spain was covered by sea and then many millions of years later, about 10 million years ago, the European and African plates collided causing the uplift and folding of rock layers. Faults occurred much later on when individual massifs were created (e.g. Montgó) that have retained their current appearance for 1.6 million years. The area of the Marina Alta mountains is a karst region with many springs and dry gorges created by fierce erosion and the province of Alicante is dominated by the Sierra de Aitana with a height of 1558m, the highest range in the region and the northeastern tip of the Baetic Cordillera, a mountain system stretching northeastwards from southern Spain. The land drops steeply down on its south side forming an abrupt change in landscape profile. Steeply rising narrow limestone ridges extend eastwards as far as the sea and drop down in spectacular steps into the water (e.g. the Sierra de Bèrnia).

The landscape of Alicante's interior is characterised by innumerable terraces that were skillfully designed by the Moors who were inherent experts in agriculture and irrigation. The construction of terraces had its heyday in the 17/18th centuries when an increase in population and shortage of land made it necessary to make optimum use of agricultural areas. Since the Costa Blanca is a region of limestone, there are many springs and dry gorges which have been eroded over the centuries.

Flora

Spain is blessed with an extraordinarily diverse flora, much greater than in any other European country. The large number of different natural habitats allows many endemic species. Alicante has a typical Mediterranean vegetation of bushes, but by the rivers and in the cooler mountain areas you will also find a vegetation of middle-European origin, e.g. ferns or mixed forests of field maple, poplar and ash. For a Mediterranean landscape, there is an amazing colour change in some areas in October and November. The olive

Many walks are also suitable for elderly people.

and the kermes oak are also characteristic species of the evergreen decidu-ous range, as well as the strawberry tree, box and mock privet. Two species of pine tree are prevalent, the Aleppo pine and the stone pine. The stone pine with its unmistakable shape and the olive and cypress trees are charac-teristic of the Mediterranean area. Old stands of olives form thin groves in between which, on fallow ground, you might come across wild orchids. Among the typical vegetation is the up to 6m tall macchia consisting of the mastic tree, Phoenician juniper, kermes oak, carob, oleander and terpentine tree. The lower scrub, up to 1m tall, consists of spurge, gorse (e.g. blue hedgehog broom, at higher altitudes), dwarf fan palms, the white and pink rock roses and herbs like rosemary and thyme, as well as many types of heather (e.g. Spanish heather, *Erica australis*), all of which can withstand the long hot summers. The American agave characterises the landscape espe-cially inland together with the hedgehog cactus, which was introduced by Spanish explorers, with its unexpectedly edible fruits. Canarian date palms (*Phoenix canariensis*) are popular ornamental plants and, of course, the bright, usually pinky-purple bougainvillea; red carpobrotus, a favourite suc-culent, stabilises hillsides and dunes near the sea. Market gardens at the coast with swathes of netting covering fruit trees (orange, lemon, medlar) extend over the fertile plains, e.g. in the Guadalest valley, while almond trees, olive trees and carob dominate the expertly constructed terraces in dry moun-tain areas. Cherries are cultivated at higher altitudes and harvested in May. Almond and olive growing is very important in the province of Alicante and

Luxuriant vegetation in the Guadalest valley.

viticulture is a significant industry, particularly in the Vinalopó and Jalón valleys (the Moscatel sweet wines are to be recommended) where you can taste the wines in the bodegas (wine cellars).

Fauna

On some of the walks you will come across the tracks made by wild boar. The animals themselves are very rarely seen, although you might possibly glimpse them at sunset. Amongst the larger mammals are fox, deer and mountain goats. The sunny rock slopes are home to many reptiles, including small lizards and snakes, of which a few are poisonous, but not deadly. Hundreds of butterflies are a delight from May to October especially, the most distinctive being the brilliant yellow Cleopatra, the Swallowtail and the Two-tailed Pasha.

Birds of prey include buzzards, kestrels and Bonelli's eagles (Spain has about 70% of the European population although their numbers are on the decline). Peregrines and griffon vultures have been reintroduced into the Barranc del Sinc. Golden eagles are widespread, but are seen only fleetingly. Black choughs live in the high mountain areas and are recognisable by their throaty calls. The hoopoe that lives all year round in open woodland is a stunning sight with its startling black and white plumage. The nightingale sings in spring and summer, nesting in the dense vegetation of bushy gardens and thickets. You can hear little owls from April to August, calling like cats at dusk, and the bee-eater that you may see and hear from May to September is one of the most colourful birds in Europe. It has a distinctive reedy burbling, but far-reaching, call. Flamingos and other waders in the wetlands are also of interest to enthusiastic birdwatchers.

Protection of nature and the environment

Some nature reserves have been set up in the province of Alicante for the protection of ecosystems, plants and birdlife – Montgó, Peñón de Ifach, Salinas de Santa Pola, El Hondo, Salinas de la Mata, Font Roja and Sierra Mariola and most recently the Sierra Helada. Microreservas are small areas of under 20 hectares that are home to rare botanical species, endemic and introduced, or even outstanding examples like huge trees. You will come across some of these small areas of conservation on walks around the Sierra de Bèrnia (Walk 13) and on the Sierra de Aitana (Walk 28). There are also three wetland areas (*humedales*) in the south of the province: the natural parks of las Lagunas de la Mata, El Hondo and Las Salinas de Santa Pola are home to a large variety of birdlife.

Please respect all plant and animal life. Do not leave litter behind and due to the acute danger of forest fire, especially in the dry summer months, do not light a fire in the open and never throw cigarette ends onto the ground. In the summer there is a general fire ban in country areas until November.

Pozos de nieve – snowpits

Some of the walks (e.g. Walks 28, 42 and 43) go past one or more snow pits, called *pozos de nieve* in Spanish. From the 16th to the 19th century snow was packed into the pits to make ice for the preservation of food, cold drinks and medicinal purposes, but with the advent of industrial ice towards the end of the 19th century snow pits fell into disuse and the tradition was lost. These fascinating constructions (also called *nevera*, *cava* or *clos*) were built chiefly at altitudes of over 800m on the north side of the mountains near to significant trade routes. Their walls were reinforced with stonework and a stone roof protected it from the sun. Often a small house belonging to the keeper of the snow (*nevatero*) was built nearby. The ice that was formed was put onto the backs of mules and carried into the valleys at night, although, depending on the distance, condition of the paths and weather, 20 to 50 percent of it was lost.

History of the Moors in Spain

The Moors who came from North Africa dominated events on the Iberian peninsula for centuries. They invaded the Christian Spain of the Visigoths through Gibraltar in 711 and rapidly conquered Portugal and large areas of the Spain of today except for a few pockets in the northwest and the Basque regions in the Pyrenees.

The Reconquista, the reconquering of Moorish occupied territory which lasted almost 750 years, began in 722 with the battle of Covadonga (Asturia) between Asturian-Cantabrian Christians and Moors, and did not end until 1492 with the fall of Granada. Nevertheless towns such as Granada, Seville and Córdoba enjoyed an unequalled period of prosperity under Moorish rule. After 1492 most Muslims had to convert to Christianity and were called *morisicos*. The Arabs were tolerated up until 1609 when they had to leave the country. Most of the Morisco population was to be found in what is called Andalucía today as well as in the east of the peninsula, in the kingdom of

Valencia, where they accounted for about a third of the population until the 17th century. In the Valencian Community the innumerable terraced fields, the network of paths and irrigation systems are, to this day, a sign of the Moors' expert agricultural knowledge. The names of some villages date back to the Moors, e.g. Beniali ('beni' means 'son of', although the origin of Benidorm's name is still unknown) and Alicante (Al-Akant).

Mozarabs were Christians who kept their religion and lived under Islamic rule until the end of the 11th century. They influenced a style of art and architecture (like Catholic churches with horseshoe arches). Mudejar was the name given to those Moors who were allowed to keep their religion after the Reconquista at a time when there was religious tolerance and everyone was allowed to practise their beliefs. This resulted in individual artistic, architectural and literary styles. The Mudéjar style is characterised by the use of brick as the most important building material. It also combines elements of Christian architecture with Islamic ornaments. The final expulsion of the Moors took place in 1609 which caused a serious setback for the economy and culture of Spain.

The limestone massif of Montgó between Dénia and Xàbia (Walk 1).

Alicante

The capital of Alicante province has a lot to offer the tourist including a walk along the colourful and very popular Explanada. The three-coloured marble floor was constructed in 1958 and four rows of palms, two on each side, border a central promenade. Take a stroll here in the early evening past elegant buildings, visit the various stalls selling leather, craft goods and jewellery and sit at one of many cafés to choose from (beware of bag-snatchers). One of the best museums is the *Museo de Arte Contemporáneo de Alicante* (MACA, Museum of Contemporary Art) with works by Picasso, Miró, Dalí, Kandinsky, Max Ernst and many more. The town hall with its magnificent portal and twin towers in the old quarter behind the Explanada at its northern end is a Baroque masterpiece. The castle of Santa Bárbara, from which you can enjoy a wonderful view across the whole bay and town of Alicante, is one of the largest medieval fortresses in Europe. The castle is accessible by a lift which you access through a 205m tunnel in the rock. Return down through the castle and descend the new and attractively designed pathway into the narrow streets of the old town and eventually to the town hall. Street markets are held on Thursdays and Saturdays (8–14.00), e.g. in Benalúa on Avenida Catedrático Soler. (For a visit of the town it's best to drive as far as the harbour and park in the underground car park next to Hotel Meliá. From here the Explanada, the old town and the lift to the castle are easily accessed.) From the *Estación de Autobuses* situated to the south of the harbour there's a regular bus service to the airport (Information at tel.: 00 34/965 130 700.

Tourist office: Rambla Méndez Núñez, 23, tel.: 00 34/965 200 000. On the internet: www.alicanteturismo.com.

Alicante town hall.

General information

Spanish Tourist Office, 64 N Row London W1K 7DE, tel.: 020 7317 2011. There are a variety of useful websites on the internet, www.spain.info, www.comunitatvalenciana.com, www.costablanca.org and www.infocostablanca.com. Local tourist offices

The atmosphere is very relaxed out of season on the former pirate island of Tabarca.

also offer maps, leaflets and brochures about walks and places of interest in the area.

The English speaking weekly newspaper Costa Blanca News (www.costa-news.com) is published once a week on a Friday and available from most paper shops in larger towns. It contains all you need to know about weekly markets, buses, local events etc.

Getting there

By plane: Alicante airport is a popular destination for most flight operators. The airport is 12km away from the town centre (Information: www.aena-aeropuertos.es). Taxis into the centre of Alicante cost around 19 euros. There is a regular bus to Benidorm, Altea, Calp, Dénia, Torrevieja, Elche and Murcia www.resorthoppa.com/alicantetransfers.asp and www.alsa.es). For the northern tourist resorts you can fly to Valencia, and for the most southerly, fly to Murcia airport at San Javier on the coast.

Trains: Alicante is connected with all the most important Spanish and European towns by trains of the Spanish railway company RENFE (Red Nacional de Ferrocarriles Españoles, www.renfe.es). Travelling by rail is relatively cheap; tickets are available from larger train stations and also in travel agencies in larger towns, otherwise from the conductor. The tram, TRAM Metropolitano de Alicante (known as Trenet) connects the coastal towns between Alicante and Dénia (www.discover-alicante.com/trams/alicante-trams.html and www.tramalicante.es). The journey takes rather a long time (e.g. Alicante-Dénia takes almost 3 hrs. with changes).

Car: you can drive to the Costa Blanca region along the A-7, Autopista del Mediterráneo (tolls). The N-332 runs parallel to the Alicante coast and links the most important towns of Dénia, Altea, Benidorm, Alicante and Torrevieja while the N-340 links Alicante to Elche and Alcoy inland.

Theft

As in all larger European towns you need to take great care of your personal belongings and guard against pick-pocketing and having your car broken into. Unfortunately there are many instances of bags being snatched in even the busiest spots in Alicante. There are usually no problems in the countryside, but never leave valuables in your car.

Bank holidays

The following festivals (*dias festivos*) are celebrated throughout Spain: 1.1., 6.1. (*Reyes Magos*, Three Kings), Good Friday, 1.5., 15.8. (*Asunción de la Virgen María*, Assumption), 12.10. (*Día de la Hispanidad*, in honour of Columbus' arrival in America), 1.11. (*Todos los Santos*, All Saints), 6.12. (*Día de la Constitución*, Constitution Day), 8.12. (*Inmaculada Concepción*, Immaculate conception), 25.12. Info: www.costablanca.org.

Perhaps the most popular festival (*fiesta*) in this region of Spain is the *Moros y Cristianos* (Moors and Christians), where, in more than 50 communities on the Costa Blanca, the memory of the Islamic past is celebrated. The festival in Villajoyosa (the 'joyful town') is one of the oldest of its kind and its highpoint is the landing of the Moors, an event that has been taking place in the early hours of the morning on 28 July for over 200 years. However, Alcoi is the undisputed capital of the *Moros y Cristianos* and this spectacular experience takes place in April in honour of Saint George – probably the most colourful, and certainly the noisiest, with wonderful processions, traditional dances and staged battles between the Moors and Christians with loud volleys of gunfire. The following fiestas are also worth mentioning: in Biar (May) with the curious Mohammedan figure, the Mahoma; night processions in Villena (September); the bonfires of St. John, *Les Fogueres de Sant Joan* (June in Alicante); carnival and the *Fallas* in Benidorm (15–19 March); *Semana Santa* (Holy Week) in Alicante and Orihuela at Easter. There are also numerous local fiestas in honour of the Patron Saints of villages (*fiestas patronales*). These festivals are based on strong traditional customs such as processions with the statue of the Patron Saint through the village, accompanied by the village band, the giant paella for everyone in the village square, but also dances, processions in traditional dress, concerts, fireworks and generally lots of loud bangs.

Hunting season

The hunting season, depending on the type of hunt, lasts from the middle of July until the beginning of February. They hunt mostly red-legged partridge and rabbits (also wild boar and deer in some areas, e.g. Sella). For safety reasons private hunting land is marked with black and white signs with the words *coto privado de caza* (in Valencian *caça*). You should be particularly careful when out walking during the main season (12 Oct.–6 Dec.).

Climate

The Costa Blanca coast has a mild Mediterranean climate. The average temperature is 13 °C in winter and 24 °C in summer. Most days of rain occur in March/April and September/October. However, the Costa Blanca is also suffering a climate change which is having its effect on the region with sudden spells of frost in winter and an increase in precipitation in spring. The weather is becoming more unpredictable, as it is everywhere, and the sun is much stronger. In winter (especially January/February) it can be very cold and windy at the coast while in the mountains – even in those close to the coast such as the Sierra de Bèrnia – snow is not a rarity these days. In the spring and summer it is recommended that you take sun cream with you on your walks as well as a showerproof jacket and warmer clothing. In July and August it is necessary to use a strong sun screen (also sun glasses and a sunhat/cap) and drink plenty of liquids. Avoid the midday sun if at all possible.

Markets

A small market with stalls selling mainly fruit and vegetables takes place at least once a week in most villages while all major towns have a weekly street market. Market days can be found in the Costa Blanca News (see General information).

Opening times

Smaller shops are mostly open 9–14.00 (Mon–Sat) and 17–20.30 (Mon–Fri). Bakers also open on Sunday mornings. Supermarkets have longer opening hours – they open mostly all day and sometimes on Sunday in summer (most need photo ID if paying with a credit card). Large shopping centres and department stores in Alicante open all day, in summer up until midnight sometimes. Tourist offices in smaller towns are usually open only in the morning and afternoon but are mostly shut at the weekend. Museums and historic buildings are normally closed on Mondays. Banks open 8.30–14.00 (Mon–Fri), post offices (*correos*) 8.30-14.30 (Mon–Fri, in larger towns like Alicante and Benidorm 8.30-20.30), 9.30-13.00 (Sat). Many restaurants in the country are only open at midday, at weekends or in summer also in the evening sometimes, and often close on Monday.

Climate table for the Costa Blanca (average temperatures)												
Month	1	2	3	4	5	6	7	8	9	10	11	12	Year
Temperature °C	11	12	14	16	19	22	25	25	23	19	15	12	18
Hours of sunshine	178	181	226	243	288	308	341	308	254	225	181	169	242
Precipitation (mm)	20	27	25	34	32	22	4	8	41	66	42	34	30

Language

There are two official languages in the community of Valencia: Castilian (High Spanish) and Valencian. Linguistically Valencian is a variety of Catalan, but Valencians consider it a language in its own right. It has its own vocabulary, as well as its own grammar and pronunciation. Valencian is mainly spoken in villages, but Castilian is also used or at least understood. Regional languages were prohibited under Franco, although they always prevailed, particularly in the country and with older people. After Franco's time, when the various regions received autonomous status, emphasis was given once more to individual cultures and regional languages. This is why so much importance is laid upon it today and it is taught in schools, and many young people are once again speaking Valencian amongst themselves. Indeed, you need to pass a language test in Valencian if you want to take up an official post in the region.

The beautiful flowering Spanish foxglove in spring which is only found on the Iberian peninsula.

Walking signposts mainly use Valencian names, however, the place names on the 1:50,000 maps are in Castilian Spanish. The maps to a scale of 1:50,000 and 1:25,000 are the basis for the small maps in this guide. In the walk descriptions a mixture of both Valencian and Castilian is used depending on which names are more common in a particular area. The names are usually very similar and are rarely confusing, but special mention is made when the spelling is very different, i.e. Jávea/Xàbia. A glossary at the end of the book provides some useful vocabulary for walkers in Castilian, Valencian and English.

Telephone

The country code for Spain is 00 34; from Spain to England 00 44. There's generally good coverage for mobile telephones, but not always a signal in remoter areas. The central number for an emergency is 112 (operators also offer support in English, French and German).

Karstic limestone paths and caves above Dénia

The impressive profile of Montgó, sometimes likened to the head of an elephant, runs parallel to the coastline and drops down in the east to the Cape of San Antonio. Montgó was declared a nature reserve in 1987. It extends across the communities of Dénia and Xàbia and with a surface area of 2118 hectares, is home to an interesting botanical diversity with over 650 species, many of them endemic.

Starting point: Plana de Justa, 220m. From Xàbia (Jávea) northwards along the CV-736 towards Dénia, turn left a good way after the 6km stone (sign for the »Camp de Tir Les Planes Dénia«, shooting range, not the »Campo de Tiro« 200m beforehand), drive 200m to a barrier; park here.
Height difference: 820m.
Grade: steep ascent across the northeast face, exposed section of path before the summit, sharp-edged limestone rocks on narrow paths across the top. Some PR-CV 152 waymarkers.
Maps: IGN-CNIG 822-II/823-I.
Food/accommodation: in Dénia, Xàbia.

Worth seeing: Gata de Gorgos near Xàbia (a range of shops with baskets, wickerwork, furniture and objects made from cane and bamboo).
Alternatives: 1. Alternative start: from Plaça Jaume I in Dénia along Av. Montgó to the Carretera Colonia del Montgó, along here to the right up through the forest as far as the info board at the entrance to the nature reserve.
2. At Camino de Colonia (9) turn left to Dénia (½ hr.) and take a taxi back to the Camp de Tir to avoid the 4km walk back.
Tip: start early in order to avoid a strenuous ascent in the fierce midday heat.

From the **car parking area (1)** head towards the mountain along a track lined with cypress trees, dwarf fan palms and from May to Oct. Friar's cowl. After just under 10 mins. turn right and a few mins. later continue straight on past a left hand turn-off. Ignore a right hand turn-off to the Cova del Camell (**2**; your return route) and then at an info board after about 15 mins. from the start bear right up a narrow path over sharp limestone, a typical feature of this walk. At a signposted junction go left (**3**: another path from the Cova comes up from the right). Old red dots and new yellow and white markers guide you up the zigzag path. A long steep ascent, with some scrambling

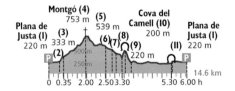

Marvellous views down to Xàbia and the sea before the summit of Montgó.

and a very exposed section, brings you to the big cairn on **Montgó's summit (4)** after about 2 hrs. You are rewarded with a spectacular panorama of the mountains inland and of the whole of the Gulf of Valencia to the north as far as Oropesa. From the summit continue straight ahead down the main path (where you need to be careful over the sharp rocks). A little later a path goes off right at a solitary tree to the Creueta de Dénia, 713m, and returns to the main path 20 mins. further down. Continue downhill a long way

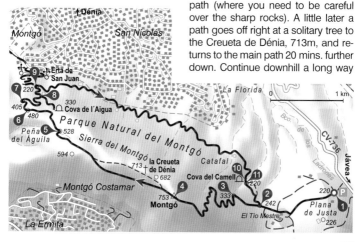

Along the top of Montgó.

through spectacular mountain scenery until the narrow path eventually ascends again and winds its way through low dwarf palms to swing right and cross the top of a **barranco (5)** to reach another solitary pine tree.

Just 10 mins. later you come to a signpost (**6**; carry straight on to Jesús Pobre) which directs you very steeply (in places almost vertically) down to the right towards Dénia. The well made path is covered in loose stones in the upper section and zigzags downhill over rock steps. Red valerian, honeysuckle and white daisies line the path. Turn right when you meet another **path (7)** about 20 mins. after the signpost. A good 800m along this initially level path you come to the **turn-off right (8)** up to the **Cova de l'Aigua** which is hidden in the rock. A Roman inscription in the rock just to the left of the entrance dates the cave to 238 AD when there was a military post here for the purpose of watching over the coast. At one time water was collected in a cistern in the cave and piped to Dénia, but there's no sign of water today. Iberian, Roman and Arabic ceramics have been found in the cave. From the **turn-off (8)** continue down the long zigzag path until, after about

A prominent waymarker – the solitary pine tree before the descent towards Dénia.

another 10 mins., you reach the broad **Camino de la Colonia (9)**, where you turn right (left to Dénia, see Alternative). With wonderful views down across the coastline of Montgó and towards the Cabo de San Antonio follow the 4km long balcony path virtually on the level to the **Cova del Camell (10)**. The broad path narrows just before the cave. Ascend the rocks to the right of the cave and after reaching the top carry straight on **(11)**. Take the left fork at a junction soon after and pass a trig point. The path soon brings you downhill to the track **(2)** that leads back left to the **starting point (1)**.

Ancient sculpted steps and water-sculpted rocks

This walk is a variation on the classic PR-CV 147 known as 'La Catedral de senderismo'. The 'Cathedral' or 'Queen of walks' as it is also known, is one of the most beautiful walks in the community of Valencia. While the descent through the Barranc d'Infern (Hell's gorge) is only recommended for experienced climbers with the appropriate equipment, this route takes you down a beautiful and ancient stepped trail into the bottom of the Río Girona valley and along the dry riverbed to the entrance to the ravine to explore the pools and the end of the abseil route. From the riverbed you return on a different route that takes you up along an airy path across the steep hillside with views down into the Barranc d'Infern to meet another beautifully constructed stepped path that continues uphill towards the village of Benimaurell.

Starting point: Fleix, 438m. West along CV-721 from Orba via Campell to Fleix. Drive up through the village and after a sharp right hand bend park on the right in front of the school (2 walking info boards).
Height difference: 480m.
Grade: clear paths and unsurfaced roadways, but tiring ascent to Benimaurell; clambering over boulders in the riverbed; some yellow and white waymarkers.
Map: IGN-CNIG 822-I.
Food/accommodation: bars in Fleix and Benimaurell. Hotel Restaurante Alahuar just outside Benimaurell (tel.: 0034/ 965 583 397, www.hotelalahuar.com), Venta El Collao restaurant on the Collado de la Garga to the west of Benimaurell.
Worth seeing: 1. Spectacular drive to Vall d'Ebo, a small village with ethnological museum: from Orba on the CV-715, then left onto the CV-712.

2. Cova del Rull (amazing, colourful stalagmites and stalactites, discovered in 1919: from Vall d'Ebo 1.5km in the direction of La Vall d'Alcalá).
3. Pla de Petracos, cave paintings north of Castell de Castells towards Vall d'Ebo.
Alternative: 1. You can extend the walk with a detour eastwards along the riverbed to the Embalse de Isbert, an old reservoir, 50 mins. there and back.
2. Ascend the steps straight on from the riverbed and follow the PR-CV 147 before returning to Benimaurell via Juvees de Dalt (walking board and waymarkers).
Tips: take plenty of water with you. This walk should not be undertaken in the height of summer due to the extreme heat in the riverbed. Walking through the gorge even several days after heavy rain can be extremely dangerous (people have died in the gorge each year).

From the school in **Fleix (1)** turn right along the road towards Benimaurell. A few paces further on take the narrow tarmac road on the right down past a **washhouse** (**2**; *lavadero*); shortly afterwards turn right down a yellow and white marked path which zigzags down a long series of shallow steps. After 20 mins. the path goes through an archway that has been blasted through the rock. As you descend (some recent erosion of the steps in places) the views open out and become even more stunning. You pass a small waterfall

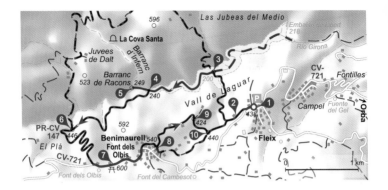

on the right which only runs water in winter and after another 20 mins. you finally reach the riverbed of the **Río Girona (3)**. A detour runs eastwards (to the right) along the riverbed to the **Embalse de Isbert**.

Turn left along the riverbed through dramatically sculpted rock formations and over smooth white boulders. Look out for a cairn in the centre of the riverbed **(4)** after about 15 mins. and two more cairns on the left which mark the start of your ascent path. Before that, however, continue along the riverbed with some scrambling over boulders to explore the start of the ravine. The beautiful oleander blossom in spring and summer makes a wonderful contrast to the white rocks. The gorge becomes narrower and you are bal-

The ancient steps lead a long way down to the riverbed.

ancing over large smooth boulders. At the point where another *barranco* comes down from the left (no access) the riverbed bends to the right and in about 10 mins. you reach the first of the pools.

Depending on the level of the water you can climb up the iron rungs and venture further into the ravine. However, you need to turn back at the end of the climbers' abseil route (**Barranc de Racons, 5**; only for experienced climbers) to return in about 20 mins. to the cairn in the middle of the riverbed **(4)** and take the narrow path on the right steeply uphill (two small orange dots) across the hillside. After a viewpoint with views down into the Barranc d'Infern continue along the increasingly narrow path which becomes rather exposed across the slope covered in

Waves of white rock in beautiful contrast to the pink oleander.

asphodels and round to the left towards an orange-coloured rock face. The path contours round the head of a valley where it is overgrown for a short way, leads across a scree slope and then between dense dwarf fan palms. On the right you can now the stepped path that comes down from Juvees de Dalt. At the **PR-CV 147 signpost (6)** turn left towards Benimaurell and the path zig-zags for a good 30 mins. up the steps. The path descends slightly at the top until you come to a tarmac road (info board). Descend the road here to the left past the **Font dels Olbis** (7; picnic table) to reach **Benimaurell**, the so-called 'Corazón de la Cereza' (heart of the cherry-growing country).

Walk left around the top of the village and down to the right past two bars. Just after the third **bar (8)** turn sharp left. (Or take the next left downhill past a wash house and along the narrow tarmac road in about 30 mins. back to Fleix.) The concrete roadway further down bends to the right and then left, at which point you carry straight on along a **dirt track (9)** which soon narrows to a path. Turn left when you reach a T-junction **(10)** and continue gently uphill eventually past the **washhouse (2)** from the start of your walk and another 5 mins. brings you back to **Fleix (1)**.

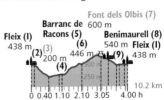

A spectacular ridge walk with historical background

Cavall Verd (Spanish Caballo Verde, Green Horse) is the Valencian name given to this ridge ends that at the Penya Roig (Spanish Peñón Rojo, red rock). The Cavall Verd is actually the easternmost part of this 6km long ridge which on the maps is also called Serra del Penyó (Spanish Sierra del Peñón). This walk leads from Benimaurell up onto the exciting ridge which looks like a saddle joining the two highest points. It is here that an historic battle took place. When Felipe II ordered the final expulsion of the Moors in 1609, the last remnants around the Vall de Laguar took shelter in the castle on Penya Roig. According to an ancient legend, a Moorish knight on a green charger was said to ride out in an attempt to save them. However, they were finally forced to surrender and were shipped to Africa from the port of Dénia. Another legend tells of their massacre on the mountain.

Starting point: Benimaurell, 540m. From Fleix (see Walk 2) continue westwards along the CV-721. Park near the fork as you enter the village.
Height difference: 370m.
Grade: easy path to the ridge, some scrambling on the second half of the ridge, waymarked yellow and white throughout as the PR-CV 181.
Map: IGN-CNIG 822-I.

Food: Bars in Benimaurell; Restaurante El Collao to the west of Benimaurell at the Collado de Garga.
Worth seeing: the Moorish steps near Fleix into the Río Girona valley (see Walk 2).
Remarks: depending on the map or signposts etc., you will find many different spellings, for example Penyó Roig instead of Penya Roig or Serra del Penyó Roig or Cavall Vert instead of Verd.

From the fork in **Benimaurell** turn left uphill (sign for the *Centre Urbà*), past a small triangular square and turn first left (**1**; PR-CV waymarker on the wall at the top of the street). Follow the road as it bends to the left, then uphill to the south to a **path (2)** turning off right (signposted to Collao de Garga; the path straight ahead also brings you up to the ridge, **5**). The path ascends ancient steps in places, at first through trees, then between terrace walls to meet a hairpin bend on the road to the Collado de Garga. Turn left up the road and after a few metres left again (signpost) up a narrow path that leads to a house. Turn right here and at a **fork (3)** ascend to the left. The path goes uphill through the terraces covered in beautiful white daisies in March. 45 mins. from the start of the walk you reach a junction on the ridge (**4**; lovely stopping point).

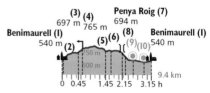

The rocky ridge section on Cavall Verd with far-reaching views of the sea.

Turn left following the sign, this time spelt 'Cavall Vert, 4.3km'. A wonderful mountain path traverses the southern hillside just below the crest of the ridge with distant views of the coast and the mountains in the south. After a good hour you reach a **signpost (5)**. Continue straight ahead where the adventure really begins.

The rest of the ridge walk requires surefootedness and is far more challenging as it continues up and down over rocks. Two places in particular require some scrambling, an uphill rock scoop and the down-climb of a **rock step (6)** protected with a rope.

Eventually you descend to a **col (7)** just before **Penya Roig** (signpost). Turn left here and descend a steep and loose path that zigzags down to an unsurfaced track. Turn left again, then immediately right before a **barrier (8)** onto a narrow path that winds steeply downhill to a surfaced roadway. Turn left at the bottom and follow this road, after about 400m past the **Font del Penyó (9)**, to meet the CV-721 road coming from Fleix at the **Font del Cambesot (10)**. Turn left along this road which brings you gradually uphill in about 15 mins. (750m) back to **Benimaurell (1)**.

A walk onto a beautiful ridge in remote countryside

La Vall d'Alcalá was the centre of Al-Azraq's resistance to Jaume I in the 13th century. This walk leads past the ruins of a Moorish village, ascends the Serra de la Foradà (Sierra Foradada, mountain riddled with holes) to just below a rock window and continues along the ridge which was ravaged by fire in 2009.

Starting point: Alcalá de la Jovada, 638m, on the CV-712 between Planes and Vall d'Ebo; park near the swimming pool (hiking board on the corner).
Height difference: 270m.
Grade: moderate walk up and down along the ridge; few waymarkers due to fire in 2009.
Map: IGN-CNIG 821-II.
Food/accommodation: in Alcalá de la Jovada, campsite and restaurant (closed Mon), Restaurante/Bar Pepa at the swimming pool, Casa rural/restaurante La

Font d'Alcalà.
Worth seeing: 1. The ruins of L'Atzuvieta (also Adsubia; 13th century Moorish village, abandoned by the Moors in 1610, used as a corral until 18th century).
2. Nevera de Baix (well-preserved snow pit with roof, end 18th century) on the CV-712 east of Alcalá de la Jovada.
3. Bronze bust and font of Al-Azraq (his nickname refers to his blue eyes), the famous Moorish leader, in Alcalá de la Jovada.
Tip: walking poles an advantage for the descent.

From the walking sign in **Alcalá de la Jovada (1)** go northeastwards along the CV-712 and down the second road on the left **(2)**. Past the sewage works you come to **L'Atzuvieta (3)**, the best preserved Moorish settlement in the area; it's worth taking time to explore the ruins of the village. Immediately afterwards turn right along a road that is surfaced only at the start; on the right on the far side of the main road you can see the Nevera de Baix (snow pit). At a **fork (4)** ascend left up a rocky path (the path right leads to Vall d'Ebo) directly towards the mountain ridge.

At the **Mas del Metge (5**; wrongly located on most of the maps) follow the path to the right and go left at the fork up to the top of the ridge with the rock window in the Penya Forada now coming into view for the first time. At the top of the path you are afforded breathtaking views down into the Vall de Gallinera and to the right you can see the ancient Moorish stepped path down into the valley that has been cut into the rock (the PR-CV 167 leads downhill round steep bends into the valley). From here walk left to a **sign (6**; detour up to the right to rock window, la Foradà) then continue along the narrow stony path up the ridge. Descend some rock slabs to a col and head for the next rise with brilliant views of both

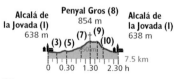

Alcalá de la Jovada (I)
638 m

Penyal Gros (8)
854 m

Alcalá de la Jovada (I)
638 m

(3) (5)   (7) (9)   (10)

7.5 km

0   0.30   1.30   2.30 h

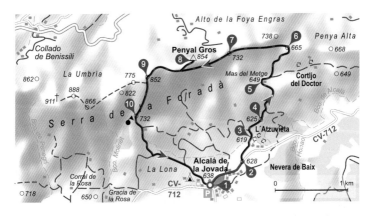

valleys. Descend once more to a **wall (7)** and on the other side continue just below the ridge line, following cairns, as you head uphill again towards Penyal Gros with its distinctive overhanging rock and caves. Follow the gently ascending path, then cut back right to find your way to the summit of **Penyal Gros** (8; 854m) where a spectacular view awaits you: to the north you can see the church tower of Alpatró down in the Gallinera valley with the Sierra de la Safor beyond, the steep peak of Benicadell to the northwest, the Serrella pinnacles and the Aitana summit in the south and on a clear day even the silhouette of Montgó in the southeast.

Now there's quite a steep ascent to negotiate before reaching the last summit where the path ends. At the **cairn (9)** turn left and walk past another cairn to the edge of the ridge. Your descent follows the spur quite steeply downhill over rough ground, and loose stones at times, as it heads towards a ruin. At the bottom veer to the right to a narrow **path (10)** which then descends left to a cement track. Continue downhill. At a junction bear left and follow the road down past the campsite to the main road and your **starting point (1)**.

View eastwards along the Serra de la Foradà.

Mills, cherry trees and a chapel

The impressive Barranco de la Encantada, the enchanted valley, lies to the northeast of Planes. On this walk you can enjoy dramatic views down into the narrow cleft of the gorge, a stroll past cherry orchards on the nearly 700m high Sierra Cantalar, views of the Embalse de Beniarrés before and after the ascent of an ancient stepped path to the delightfully situated Ermita del Santo Cristo above Planes.

Location: Planes, 449m.
Starting point: about 2km east of Planes on the CV-700, turn left just before the bridge, Pont de les Calderes, 490m; park by the side of the road.
Height difference: 320m.
Grade: easy walk with steep ascent to the Ermita and up to the col on the return.
Map: IGN-CNIG 821-II.

Food/accommodation: in Planes.
Worth seeing: 1. The chapel (19th century). 2. The picturesque village of Margarida on the CV-700. 3. The village of Planes with 11th century castle.
Tip: many of the tracks on this walk have been surfaced in the last years, however, it is still a worthwhile walk, especially in the beautiful light at the end of the day.

The walk starts on the level from an information board by the **Pont de les Calderes (1)** along the narrow tarmac road to the left of the riverbed. After about 5 mins. the road descends, past a green pool, gently down into a pretty valley that narrows to a gorge. Wild garlic grows at the side of the road and you can hear the water under the large boulders and frogs croaking in the pools. You come past a set of **steps with a handrail (2)** leading down to the river and a waterfall (you can also follow a path to the left by the river which meets a road that brings you to the junction (3) uphill to the left). As the road begins to descend steeply to the right into the bottom of the valley, take a track leading off to the left **(3)** and after a little while you pass the iron gates at the entrance to Villa Mónica. Continue down to the right along the path and at the bottom carry straight on along the edge of the field to a derelict house. Take a right fork afterwards downhill and past a small rock shelter. A narrow path leads down to an old mill, but keep straight on until the path bends right and heads towards the ruins

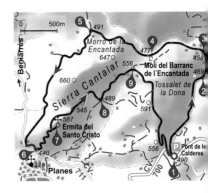

of a mill covered in ivy, **Molí del Barranc de l'Encantada (4)**. Round the back of the casita opposite there's a good viewpoint down into the deep-cut river gorge, also known as el Clot del Molí. At a fork ascend right and along the edge of the gorge through an area of honeysuckle and pink cistus to a house with a fence round it. Crag martins circle up above. Walk beside the fence past the orchards where cherries are harvested in May. You meet a surfaced track and continue uphill to a tarmac road on the **Morro de la Encantada (5)**. Turn left here with distant views to the west of the Embalse de Beniarrés and the Sierra de Benicadell beyond. The path descends in just under ½ hr. to the Planes – Beniarrés road. Go left and at the 1km stone turn back left up

Ermita del Santo Cristo.

a steep, but **stepped path (6)**, concreted at the start, that zigzags its way in 20 mins. past the Stations of the Cross up to the **Ermita de Santo Cristo (7)** with fabulous views and surrounded by cypress trees and cedars.

Now follow the tarmac road as it descends overlooking the lake and Beniarrés with its prominent church. After a ¼ hr. descent you arrive at a crossroads (**8**; information board); go left here (right goes to Planes; straight on for an alternative route not on tarmac). 10 mins. steeply uphill brings you to a **col (9)** with views northeastwards down into the gorge (a path leads back down into the *barranco*) and southwestwards of the Ermita and Planes. The road ascends again for a short way round olive and almond terraces before finally descending. The village of Catamarruc comes into view ahead. About 20 mins. after a tiny house with a palm tree (alternative route from the right joins here) you eventually reach the main road. Turn left here back to the **Pont de les Calderes (1)**.

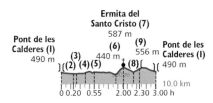

Ermita del Santo Cristo (7)
587 m

Pont de les Calderes (I)
490 m

(3)   (6)   (9)
(2) (4)(5)   440 m   556 m

Pont de les Calderes (I)
490 m

(8)

10.0 km

0 0.20 0.55   2.00 2.30 3.00 h

Retracing an old railway line beside the river

The walk begins by following the banks of the Río Serpis on the track of an old railway line that was built by an English firm in 1893 and known as the 'Tren de los Ingleses', train of the English. It ran through 8 tunnels and was used to transport goods from the industrial town of Alcoi (production of cigarette papers amongst others) to the port in Gandía. The railway line was abandoned in 1969 and dismantled. This walk goes through a tunnel, ascends the steep wooded slopes of the Sierra de la Safor, then returns through a dry streambed to L'Orxa.

Starting point: L'Orxa (also Lorcha), 262m. Walking board on the CV-701 on the eastern side of the village. Drive eastwards from Muro de Alcoy or from the south over the mountains of the Vall de Gallinera.
Height difference: 450m.
Grade: strenuous ascent to the ridge; narrow stony path beside and at times in the streambed. PR-CV 207 yellow and white waymakers.
Map: IGN-CNIG 795-IV.
Food/accommodation: in L'Orxa; swimming pool; www.casarurallatrinquetera.es.
Worth seeing: the Moorish Castell de Perputxent from the 12/13th century.

From the walking board in **L'Orxa (1)** follow the main road for about 1km down to the **bridge (2)**. Just after the bridge turn right towards the Castell de Perputxent and pass an old paper factory on the left. The dirt path beside the river brings you to the old **railway track (3)** beside the Río Serpis. Turn right and continue beside the river through a dramatic landscape (look out for little egrets) and after about 1 hr. from the start of the walk you reach a **tunnel (4)**. You pass an old water control station before eventually reaching a **fork (5)** where you descend right to the **Fábrica de la Llum (6)**. Cross over the river, ascend to the left and after a few paces turn up right (sign, straight on to Villalonga) onto a narrow path that quickly gains height and zigzags steeply uphill between dwarf fan palms and tree heather. The path is very eroded in places and you need to keep your eyes open for the twists and turns, usually waymarked. A level section of path affords a view of Benicadell to your right, then it's roughly 30 mins. steeply uphill again to a wide bend in the **forest track (7**; down right to *refugio* at the Font de la Serquera). Ascend the rough forest track as it winds steeply up round long bends until you finally reach the top, 2.2km from the refugio. Now it's a comfortable stroll to the right along a level tarmac road. Just under 15 mins. later you reach the **signpost (8)** for the **Font dels Olbis**. Cross the road and follow the track to the **picnic area (9)** in a beautiful location. Walk straight past the spring and go up

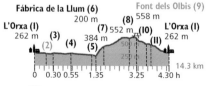

Fábrica de la Llum (6)   Font dels Olbis (9)
            200 m   558 m
L'Orxa (I)   (8)
262 m   (3)   (7) 552 m (10)   L'Orxa (I)
    (2)   (4) 384 m   (11)   262 m
                  (5)

0   0.30 0.55   1.35   3.25   4.30 h   14.3 km

two steps. The yellow and white waymarkers continue up the steps to eventually reach the summit of La Safor (1½ hrs.), but you turn right (also waymarked) along a narrow dirt path on the level which soon zigzags downhill over loose stones into the **Barranc de Bassiets** where you cross over the dry streambed. Eventually you meet a **roadway** (**10**; left to the Font dels Bassiets, 15 mins.). Turn right uphill for about 5 mins. until you come to a turn-off left below the **Casa del Felsonar (11)** which descends a steep section of rock at the start, but later runs comfortably along beside a steep-sided gorge. The path

On the banks of the Río Serpis.

then zigzags downhill again to a dry streambed. Cross the streambed and ascend the path on the other side. Follow the path which is eroded in places and occasionally gets lost and runs a couple of times through the streambed itself. After a longer section in the streambed through trees the stones come to a sudden end and you are walking across muddy ground through bushes and come out onto a large open flat area. Head straight towards the dam wall and ascend the steps on the left by the wall. Turn right down the track back to **L'Orxa (1)**.

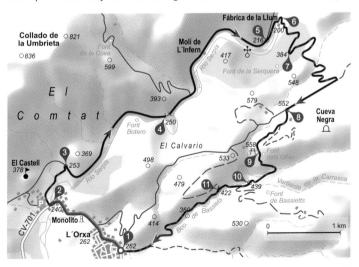

Leisurely walk in impressive mountain scenery around Tárbena

A piece of Mallorca can be found here amidst spectacular mountain scenery: after the expulsion of the Moors in 1609 wide stretches of land on the Iberian peninsula were abandoned. The problem was solved in Tárbena with settlers from Mallorca who were brought over onto the mainland in two campaigns (1612 and 1616). Their heritage is still alive today in language and traditions. The walk follows an ancient stepped pathway up to the Moorish castle built in the eleventh century and finally leads west to the site of an Iberian settlement on the impregnable La Montaña with a breathtaking view down into the Pas Tancat.

Starting point: Tárbena, 562m, car park by the Casa de Cultura. From the coast drive along the CV-715 via Callosa d'en Sarrià and Bolulla; as you reach the village turn left on a sharp right hand bend (info sign).
Height difference: 320m.
Grade: easy with some short, steep ascents and descents, yellow dots as waymarkers in the second half.

Map: IGN-CNIG 822-III.
Food: Sa Cantarella bar-rest. on the left just before entering the village with beautiful terrace and Can Pinet in the village.
Worth seeing: 1. Village of Bolulla. 2. Les Fonts de l'Algar (source area of the Algar, swimming, see Walk 12).
Remarks: PR-CVs 145 and 146 also start from Tárbena (moderate, both about 5 hrs., see info board).

Turn left out of the car park in **Tárbena (1)** and walk down the road to the info board. Turn left up the main road towards Pego for about 5 mins. until you see a **sign (2)** on the right hand side to 'Sa Caseta des Moros'. About 50m up the concrete roadway turn right in front of the large new building (**3**; sign on the wall 'Comidas, 30m'). Continue round to the left and walk past restaurant Can Pelut on your right and very soon afterwards step up left onto a narrow path. The beautiful stepped path brings you after about 1km to the **Castell dels Moros (4)**. At a fork head left towards the remains of a tower and climb up a steep, rough path to reach the site of the ancient castle with its cistern, 694m. From here you can enjoy a 360 degree panorama of the surrounding mountains: the Sierra de Bernia in the southeast and the Aitana range in the southwest, and the coastline between Altea and Benidorm.

Return to the **main road (2)**, cross straight over and follow the road uphill towards Castell de Castells. Just over 50m later on turn left onto a concrete track (start of the yellow dots) which soon narrows to a path

Distant views southwards across Tárbena to a hazy sea.

and comes down to the road again for a short while. At a right hand bend take the fourth track on the left going uphill **(5)**. Walk past a newly renovated house (El Serral) with a semi-circular balcony and continue along a narrow path which contours across the hillside with stunning views. You can see your return path, a red dirt track, below on the left.

The path swings round to the left as it ascends, then descends past a corral to a **col** (**6**; 629m). A short path takes you down to the right to a breathtaking view southwestwards into the Pas Tancat way below. A narrow rocky path continues uphill from the col onto **La Montaña (7)** and affords views this time down to the east and of the coast. Return to the **col (6)**, turn down right onto an almond terrace and find a gravel track off to the left that zigzags steeply downhill, keeping a lookout for yellow dots. At a fork turn right downhill, then look for a waymarker guiding you left. Very quickly turn right onto a terrace which contours to an arched **spring (8)**. Turn left up constructed steps until the path continues on the level round the hillside. At the next yellow dot follow the wooded path left which emerges later onto open terraces. The path swings left and descends a steep cemented track into the village. At the bottom turn left and ascend past Can Pinet bar to the **car park (1)**.

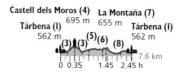

41

Peaceful walk to two spectacular natural arches

The drive alone from the coast on a winding road to the start of this walk is quite breathtaking with distant views inland and down to the sea. The route takes you through an ancient agricultural countryside to Els Arcs: two huge limestone arches, joined by a narrow bridge which nature has sculpted from the rock over millions of years.

Starting point: Pla de Dalt, 730m. Pla de Dalt, 730m. Via Callosa d'En Sarrià, Bolulla and Tárbena, then about 6km on CV-752 in the direction of Castell de Castells, left onto an unsurfaced track by the walking sign (Font dels Teixos); park here.
Height difference: 220m.
Grade: Good, broad unsurfaced tracks and paths, narrow rocky path from the turn-off to Els Arcs. PR-CV 151, yellow and white waymarkers.

Map: IGN-CNIG 848-II.
Food/accommodation: in Castell de Castells and Tárbena.
Worth seeing: 1. Pinturas rupestres at Pla de Petracos (cave paintings north of Castell de Castells).
2. Les Fonts de l'Algar between Callosa d'en Sarrià and Bolulla (see Walk 12).
Remarks: the PR-CV 49 'Senda Vella' leads on the other (north) side to Castell de Castells; 4km, 1¾ hrs., easy; about 200 vertical metres.

From the walking sign at **Pla de Dalt (1)** walk up the wide track past three ancient corrals. Ignore a turning off to the right at the **Corral de Poll (2)** and walk round to the left along the metalled road until, after about 20 mins. from the start, you come to the junction with the signpost (**3**; 'Aljub del Xarquet'). Turn left here for the first detour. At a fork continue to the right and after about 250m you can see an ancient well, the **Aljub del Xarquet (4)** built into the terrace wall. Return to the junction (**3**) and continue left as the track ascends southwestwards. Cultivated fields now intermingle with natural vegetation. At the next junction the concrete roadway ascends left towards the Font dels

Teixos (see Walk 11), but turn off right here up the track to two stone *casitas* with the ruins of corrals and abundant holm oaks (**5**; 'Cruce a Els Arcs'). Follow the dirt track to the left which narrows to a path after 150m with views across the Barranc de les Foies of Castell de Castells with the airy Penya del Castellet (see Walk 10) rising up behind, and Malla de Llop (1360m). Continue below the overhanging, ivy-covered

rock faces of the Sierra which brings you to the rock arches of **Els Arcs (6)** in an hour from the start. Look out for the pretty Star of Bethlehem which blossoms in May along the path.

Els Arcs (6)   Penya Escoda (8)
850 m   731 m
Pla de Dalt (I)   (3) (5)   (7)   Pla de Dalt (I)
730 m   (4)   (9) 730 m

6.8 km
0 0.25 1.10 1.45 2.15 h

Return to the junction **(5)** and turn left. After a short ascent you begin a gentle descent past the ruins of an enormous corral to the 'Cruce a la Penya Escoda' (**7**; 769m). Turn left and walk downhill for about 150m to the **Penya Escoda** (**8**; 731m) with its panoramic view to the west (info board). Return to the junction **(7)** and carry straight on. When you reach another junction just after the **Corral del Pi Bertol (9)** turn left to continue on the level past a plantation of fruit trees to the main road. Turn right here back to the **Pla de Dalt (1)**.

The highlight of the walk – the spectacular rock arches of Els Arcs.

9 *Pla de la Casa, 1379m*

An interesting walk to a remote snow pit

This walk brings you onto a beautiful panoramic summit in the Sierra de Serrella.

Starting point: Quatretondeta, 622m. On the CV-70 Benidorm – Alcoi road northwards as far as Benilloba, then right onto the CV-710 towards Gorga and east to Quatretondeta. About 300m after the entrance to the village turn right by the walking info board and drive along the concrete track to another interpretive sign, 668m. Park here.
Height difference: 750m.
Grade: steep ascent from the Collado de Borrell, short, easy scramble onto the small, exposed summit rock; yellow and white PR-CV 24 waymarkers.
Map: IGN-CNIG 821-IV.
Food/accommodation: Castell de Castells. No bars in Quatretondeta. Walking holidays: www.mountainwalks.com.

Alternative: If available, leave one car in Benasau on the CV-70 and descend to Benasau. From the Collado de Borrell following the sign for the PR-CV 23 to reach a green water tank. Carry on downhill round bends for about 1.5km to a distinct left hand bend; go right here (yellow and white waymarker) and down to the edge of the village. Turn left to the CV-70; 1½ hrs. from the turn-off, 5 hrs. in total from Quatretondeta.
Tip: 1. This walk is particularly spectacular after snowfall early in the year when the snow lingers longer here on the north side of the Sierra, and you can often be walking in snow well into February.
2. The strenuous PR-CV 182 from Facheca is well recommended (difficult, 6 hrs., almost 800 vertical metre).

From the **info board (1)** continue along the concrete roadway to the first **fork (2)** after about 400m where you go left. At the next **fork (3)** take the right hand path which heads towards the pinnacles. A good hour from the start you come to the first spring, **Font de l'Espinal (4)** with info board. The track now narrows to a path and zigzags more steeply up through pine trees, crosses a scree slope and ascends a very slippery scree path to arrive at a **rock gateway (5)** and eventually **Font Roja (6; picnic tables)**.

Ignoring the PR-CV 182 signpost to Facheca (also Fageca, village 5km northeast of Quatretondeta), continue uphill to a **signpost** (**7**; right towards Benasau). Turn left here along a narrow path up to the **Collado de Borrell (8)**. A short detour goes to the right over a small col, then down left to a picnic spot with superb views of Malla de Llop, the castle ruin on Serrella and the Guadalest valley. On the right you will see an enormous natural hole in the rock in the shape of Africa.

Back on the Collado de Borrell follow the narrow path (cairn) steeply uphill on a loose path and near the top through prickly bushes. At the top you come to a **waymarker post (9)** where the path bends round to the right across the almost level high plain of Pla de la Casa (*pla* means 'flat ground' in Valen-

Snow pit below the summit.

cian) covered with spikey hedgehog broom which has a beautiful blue flower in the spring. Continue along the stony path over a small rise and down to a large **snow pit** (**10**; 1335m). The *pozo de nieve* is 11m in diameter and 13m deep. (The PR-CV 182 descends further on to the Barranco del Morro in the direction of Facheca.)

To reach the summit, follow a faint path on the far side of the *pozo* which turns right uphill. Scramble onto the rocky summit on **Pla de la Casa (11)** on good footholds, but with some exposure near the top, where there's a cross, a metal box and a book for signatures. The view extends across a series of mountain peaks – the whole of the Sierra de Aitana from Monte Ponoig to the Aitana summit and Cabeçó d'Or further south. Return the same way, but now

with completely different views, especially in the late afternoon when the setting sun brings a wonderful light onto Els Frares (the monks) as the pinnacles are called, on the north side of the Sierra de Serrella.

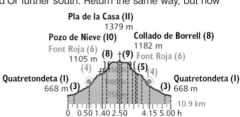

Pla de la Casa (11)
1379 m
Pozo de Nieve (10)   Collado de Borrell (8)
Font Roja (6)   1182 m
1105 m   (8) (9) Font Roja (6)
(4)   (5) (4)
Quatretondeta (1)   Quatretondeta (1)
668 m (3)   (3) 668 m
10.9 km
0 0.50 1.40 2.50   4.15 5.00 h

Exciting ascent to a castle perched high on the Sierra de Serrella

The drive from the Guadalest reservoir up to the Collado del Castellet for this walk is also an exciting experience. The route starts by contouring the northern hillside of the Sierra de Serrella with views down to Castell de Castells. It returns along the ridge offering stunning views down into the Guadalest valley and of your destination, the castle perched on top of a narrow blade of rock at the eastern end of the Sierra built by the Moors in the 13th century.

Location: Beniardà, 465m.
Starting point: Collado del Castellet, 858m. Drive along the CV-70 north from Benidorm, take the turning down right to Beniardà; at the bottom go left into the village along the narrow street, immediately right, then left steeply down to the river and over the bridge. Turn right (left to Abdet) and about 2km along the road turn second left at the PR-CV 18/19 signpost, 390m. Drive about 3km up this road, mostly tarmac or concrete (3 shortish unsurfaced sections) to the col. You can also park lower down where the tarmac ends at a pump station adding a good hour to the walk.
Height difference: 340m.
Grade: broad paths and forest tracks except for the steep ascent to the castle where there are some exposed, but easy sections of scrambling.
Maps: IGN-CNIG 821-IV/822-III.
Food/accommodation: Restaurante La

Mezquita and Bar Ça Gloria in Beniardà. Walking holidays in Abdet: www.abdet. com.
Worth seeing: the quaint old centre of Guadalest village (see also Walk 11).
Alternatives: from the starting point descend to Castell de Castells along the waymarked PR-CV 149; 1 hr., easy, about 500 vertical metres.
Linking tip: from the starting point turn right to Morro Blau (see Walk 11).
Remarks: 1. Be careful in Beniardà: you need a car no bigger than a VW Golf to drive through the narrow streets of Benihardá. 2. The Collado del Castellet can also be accessed from Castell de Castells (see Walk 11).
Tip: 1. A nice, easy walk takes you all the way round the Embalse de Guadalest (2½ hrs.). 2. After the bridge turn left up to little village of Abdet for lunch (1 hr., easy). 3. Benimantell sells very good local olive oil.

From the **Collado del Castellet (1)** carry straight on downhill for about 200m (northwards) and turn left onto broad track (**2**; sign) which crosses the top of the Barranc del Castellet. It's a lovely gentle walk as the path contours the northern hillside with views down to Castell de Castells. On a left hand bend about 1km along the track you pass the signposted **path (3)** to Castells de Castells.

A leisurely path along the ridge towards the steep Penya El Castellet with Guadalest reservoir below on the right.

After a total of ¾ hr. turn left uphill at a **fork (4)**. This forest track brings you steeply uphill round bends in just under 20 mins. to the top of the **ridge (5)** where a magnificent panorama awaits you. The view sweeps down across the Guadalest reservoir towards the sea and your destination, the former Moorish castle, appears inaccessible as it sits perched on a blade of rock ahead. (There's a cairn on the right on the col marking the start of the ascent up the Barranc de la Canal to Malla de Llop, 400 vertical metres to the summit, 1357m.) Continue downhill quite steeply and over loose stones, then it's a hefty climb up to the foot of the castle (**6**; signpost). Turn right and ascend a narrow path in just under 5 mins. to the entrance to the castle ruin and a cistern full of water on the left (be careful on the slippery grass). Take the path right that soon veers up to the left and heads for the base of the rock. From here the at times exposed path with some scrambling brings you up to the **castle (7)** itself. At the eastern end of the castle go through an archway where a fantastic view of virtually the whole of the Sierra de Aitana awaits you – the most spectacular picnic spot in the whole of the Costa Blanca!

Back down at the **signpost (6)** turn right and in about 10 mins. descend the steep track covered in loose stones to your **starting point (1)**.

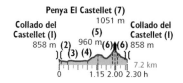

Circular walk with stunning views high up on the Sierra de Aixorta

This beautiful circular walk on the Sierra de Aixorta can be accessed from the Guadalest valley or from Castells de Castells. It starts at the Collado del Castellet and leads along a forest track on the north side of the Sierra to Morro Blau affording spectacular views both of the coast and inland. The return path leads through a remote landscape, with an optional ascent of La Xortà, to meet the forest track once more back down to the col.

Location: Beniardà, 465m.
Starting point: As in Walk 10 to the Collado del Castellet.
Height difference: 490m.
Grade: mostly clear undulating tracks as far as Morro Blau, PR-CV 150 yellow and white waymarkers in places, narrow unmarked path at times on southern side of the Sierra.
Maps: IGN-CNIG 821-IV/822-III.

Food: in Beniardà and Castell de Castells.
Worth seeing: 1. From Castell de Castells to the cave paintings at Pla de Petracos (see Walk 8). 2. Guadalest (see Walk 10).
Alternatives: 1. Alternative start from the pump station on the way from Beniardà (see Walk 10; an extra 1½ hrs. and 300m of ascent). 2. Ascent from the CV-752 near Castell de Castells (extra 1½ hrs. and 270m of ascent.

From the **Collado del Castellet (1)** walk eastwards following the PR-CV 150 in the direction of Morro Blau along a leisurely forest track with views down to Castell de Castells on your left. After about 1 hr. you reach a *casita* on a small **col** (**2**; your return path joins from the right). Carry straight on past a turning left down to the CV-752 (**3**) and a good ½ hr. later you come to a **fork** (**4**; right goes up to the Font dels Teixos with picnic tables and *refugio*). Continue left here up the concrete track (sign 'Morro Blau, 2.4km'). After a few mins. you pass a track going off left (**5**; your return route from the summit) and then after another 10 mins. you reach a col. Turn left here on a gently ascending path towards **Morro Blau (6)** with its weather station and breathtaking views of the Aitana in the southwest, the coast, Puig Campana and the Sierra Helada in the south, the Sierra de Bèrnia and Sierra del Ferrer in the east and Montgó in the northeast. Continue down the broad, scree-covered track to the east which then bends round to the left and leads in the opposite direction eventually uphill to the **junction (5)**. Turn right back to the **fork (4)** below the **Font dels Teixos**. This time walk up left to the **refugio (7)** and continue past it up the narrow, yellow

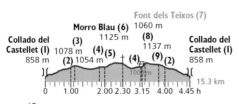

Font dels Teixos (7)   1060 m
Morro Blau (6)   1125 m   (8)
Collado del Castellet (I)   (3)   1137 m   Collado del Castellet (I)
858 m   1078 m   (4)(5)   (4)   (9)(2)   858 m
(2) 1054 m   1000 m   15.3 km
0   1.00   2.00 2.30 3.15   4.00 4.45 h

and white marked rocky path to a col on the left of La Xortà (**8**; about 15 mins. and another 100m of ascent brings you to the beautiful summit, 1219m, with extensive views). Following a red arrow to the right, look out for a blue dot on a rock on the left guiding you downhill before contouring round the hillside to the right. At a fork follow the now yellow dots left downhill through a shallow *barranco*. Across a level grassy section the rocks open out on the right to give distant views of Cocoll. Continue uphill towards a **ruin (9)** and eventually the path descends again with distant views of the Barranc de la Canal, Malla de Llop (see Walk 10) and, just to the right, the castle ruin on Penya El Castellet. The path widens as it continues downhill and eventually meets your original track on the **col (2)**. Turn left here back to your **starting point (1)** in a good ¾ hr.

View of the Bèrnia from Morro Blau.

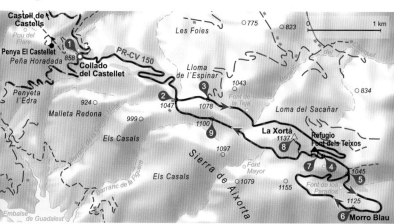

To the picturesque hamlet of Gines and along beside the Río Guadalest

Due to the abundance of water and its almost subtropical climate, Callosa d'En Sarrià in the Guadalest valley is the most important growing area for medlar fruits (Sp. níspero) in Spain. About 20 million kilos of fruit are harvested each year. The medlar which has a bitter skin was brought over to Europe from Asia in the 18th century. It is used to make jams, juices, liqueur and, more recently, beer as well and in spring is sold as fresh fruit in the markets. This walk first leads steeply up to the beautifully situated hamlet of Gines, then descends to the river with impressive views of the Sierra de Bèrnia and the coast and finally runs beside the river through orchards and medlar plantations.

Starting point: car park at the Restaurante Riu, 230m, before the bridge over the river. From Callosa d'En Sarrià drive about 4km on the CV-755 towards Guadalest.
Height difference: 220m.
Grade: easy walk, but steep ascent from the bridge up to Gines.
Map: IGN-CNIG 848-I.
Food/accommodation: Restaurante Ríu at the start; bars, restaurants in Guadalest and Callosa d'En Sarrià.
Worth seeing: 1. The pretty village of Guadalest perched high above the Embalse de Guadalest. 2. Les Fonts de l'Algar northeast of Callosa d'En Sarrià (take swimwear for a dip in the cool spring water, very busy in summer). 3. Fiesta de Moros y Cristianos, Callosa d'En Sarrià, 2nd weekend in October. 4. Local produce stall at the car park at the start.
Tip: a walk round the Guadalest reservoir on easy, broad tracks (begin at the dam, a right hand turning from the CV-755 just before Guadalest; 8km; 2½ hrs.).

From the car park at **Restaurante Riu (1)** cross over the bridge, turn left up the tarmac road (sign 'Casa Musa, 2.5km') and a 20 mins. steep ascent brings you to the road into the tiny hamlet of **Gines** (2; also Chines) which is worth a short detour. Continue round to the left uphill along the road and just under 10 mins. later turn diagonally left onto an unsurfaced track (3; sign 'Casa Musa, 1km'). The track descends in shade (ignore all turn-offs) with later views of Callosa d'En Sarrià and the prominent Bèrnia mountain ridge and the coast in the far distance. Not quite 10 mins. after the house, at the point where the track starts to ascend again, turn left **(4)**.

50

The massive Monte Ponoig; in the foreground net-covered fruit orchards and medlar plantations in the Guadalest valley.

The path can be very muddy after rain. Stay on the main path at a cross-roads and continue down past some beehives (depending on the season) on the left hand side after a warning sign *'Precaución – abejas'* (Danger – bees). Pass some more beehives on the right as the now narrower path descends beside a net-covered medlar orchard. At the bottom continue round to the right and a little later you meet the path that runs along beside the **Río Guadalest (5)**. Turn left here with bamboo and oleander by the river and medlar fruits, lemons, limes and even pomegranates growing on the left on the terraces that have been constructed with large round white river pebbles. Ignore the turn-off down across a ford on the right hand side. Up above on the right you can see a cave in the red sandstone. The path continues past a plantation of dwarf fan palms. You come to a yellow painted *finca* and another medlar plantation protected with a net. Bear left at a tall **cypress tree (6)** over the river. Now keep following the sometimes very stony path all the way back to the Pont de Gines. It crosses over the river many times, passes two water-control stations, a 'chocolate blancmange' rock and a pretty 4 storey building constructed with large river pebbles **(7)**. Look out for cattle egrets flying down the river. This riverside path is also popular with cyclists.

About ¾ hr. along this riverside path walk under the Pont de Gines, the bridge at the start of your walk, follow a path up to the left to the main road and turn left here back to the **Restaurante Riu (1)**.

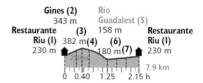

51

Through the famous 'hole' in the mountain ridge

The limestone mountain range of the Sierra de Bèrnia is a long drawn-out ridge running from southeast to northwest and forms the natural and climatic boundary between the comarcas of Marina Alta and Marina Baixa (Sp. Baja). This walk runs up across the southwestern slope to the Fort de Bèrnia, then over a picturesque col down to the Casas de Bèrnia on the northern side to then regain height up to the Forat de Bèrnia, a natural tunnel through the mountain, with stunning views across the bay of Altea as you step out onto the south side of the ridge – an exciting and very popular walk.

Starting point: Casas de Runar, 680m. Towards Callosa d'en Sarrià on CV-755 through Altea la Vella, some way past Alhama Springs take the signposted road right to the Fort de Bèrnia, go sharp right at a junction then steeply uphill round bends (some of the worst sections of the uneven road have been newly asphalted) for about 5km to a parking sign at the top. Turn left here through the houses and park at the end of the road. Alternatively you can start from the Casas de Bèrnia (6): on the CV-750 from Benissa towards Jalón, take the first road left onto the CV-749 to Pinos; turn left about 5km later at the top of the pass and park near the info board after the restaurant.

Height difference: 480m.

Grade: moderate walk on mostly good yellow and white PR-CV 7 marked path, steep ascent to the *forat* and some scrambling on the north side of the ridge just before the tunnel.

Maps: IGN-CNIG 848-I/822-III.

Food: Altea la Vella; Restaurante Bon

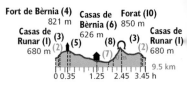

Fort de Bèrnia (4) 821 m   Casas de Bèrnia (6) 626 m   Forat (10) 850 m   Casas de Runar (1) 680 m — Casas de Runar (1) 680 m (3) (5) (2) (8) (7) (3) (2)   9.5 km   0 0.35   1.25   2.45 3.45 h

Vent on the CV-749 (open 12–15.30). Rest. Sierra Bèrnia and Rest.-Refugio Vista Bèrnia at the Casas de Bèrnia.

Worth seeing: the remains of the Fort de Bèrnia below the western summit which Felipe II had built in 1562 as a lookout post to ward off pirate attacks from the Moors, but as it was too high and too remote to be effective, it was abandoned after only 50 years.

Alternatives: ascent of the west summit of the Bèrnia, 1126m, called El Macho de la Bèrnia. From the fort walk directly uphill towards the western end of the ridge (red dots; steep ascent, airy in places, but secured with a chain where necessary; 1 hr., another 320m of ascent).

Follow the narrow path at the far end of the car park at the **Casas de Runar (1)** uphill to a signpost at the **Font del Runar (2)** where it continues sharp left. The path zigzags uphill on a good path to a scree slope and a solitary **oak tree (3)**. Walk left across the scree to the rocks (do not go directly uphill to the right towards the rock face, your descent path), then ascend the rock steps to a col. Continue along the pleasant level path to the fascinating **Fort de Bèrnia complex (4)** in ½ hr. from the start. It's worth ex-

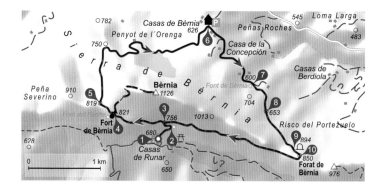

ploring the intricate ruins where you will find information boards about the history of the site (plan to spend enough time here). Continue through the ruins to the left onto a **col (5)** where you can often hear the tinkling of goat bells. From here, with Peña Severino on your left, there are spectacular views into the Algar valley of the prominent Sierra de Aixorta and Tárbena. Down to the right you can see your descent route heading for another col where the path broadens out and swings to the right with views along the Sierra de Ferrer as it runs northwards. Descend round long bends (be careful past the free-roaming bulls, keep walking, and give them a very wide berth!), past fruit orchards and down to the info board at the **Casas de Bèrnia (6)**. At the info board continue right down the road and about 15 mins. later reach the **Font de Bèrnia (7)**. The Sierra de Oltà can be seen on your left

Mist swirling above the Fort de Bèrnia.

The southern exit from the Forat de Bèrnia.

and further north along the coast, Teulada and Moraira. Montgó also comes into view in the distance to the northeast by Dénia. Turn right up the steps at the spring and walk at first comfortably, then 10 mins. later at a **fork (8)**, turn right more steeply up towards the rock face. Head left towards a prominent pine tree. Descend the path now for a short way, then it's uphill again towards a striated rock face with brambles at the bottom.

To the right and behind a huge boulder clamber up some **rock steps (9)** where you might need to use your hands. Keep close to the rock until you reach a cave which is not visible from below. Carefully make your way up a gently sloping, smooth rock slab, then continue up the now clear path to the **Forat de Bèrnia (10)**. The tunnel is just under 1m high at its lowest point so that you have to almost crawl the first 20m through to the other side where a spectacular view awaits you of the coast far below. Trailing ivy hangs across the exit from the tunnel while mist is often found swirling across the mountain. The well marked path now runs on the right parallel to the rock, up and down over scree and through dwarf fan palms (*Chamaerops humilis*) which flourish on this side of the ridge. Eventually after about 45 mins. descent you come to the **scree slope (3)** near the start of the walk. Descend left here to return to the **starting point (1)**.

Trailing ivy frames your view southwards out of the tunnel.

High on the mountain above the Costa Blanca

The Sierra de Bèrnia mountain range is a natural barrier that rises in the west up to 1126m. The walk leads up to the top of the most impressive ridge on the Costa Blanca and onto its spectacular and sheer eastern summit with breathtaking views of the coast.

Starting point: Font de Labarca, 630m. Towards Callosa d'En Sarrià on the CV-755 through Altea la Vella and just under 3km further on, past Alhama Springs urbanisation, take the road right signposted to the Fort de Bèrnia, go sharp right at a fork (arrows) then steeply uphill round bends on the uneven road for about 5km (some of the worst sections of the road have been newly asphalted). At the parking sign at the top turn right downhill (deep ruts in the road) to the parking area at Font de Labarca (barbecue site).
Height difference: 450m.

Grade: easy unsurfaced track at the start, then steep, sometimes unclear path on strenuous ascent, red and green markers and cairns in places, some exposed scrambling in the summit area, the last 20 mins. only for surefooted mountain walkers with a good head for heights.
Map: IGN-CNIG 848-I.
Food: in Altea la Vella; on the coast.
Alternative: from the starting point return along the access road to the junction, turn right as in Walk 13 to the Fort de Bèrnia (about 1¼ hrs. there and back and 140m of ascent).

Leave the barbecue site of **Font de Labarca (1)** on the right and ascend the broad forest track over a chain barrier as it runs across the hillside below the ridge and through a dense forest area (ignore all paths to the right). At the end of the just under 4km long track at the **Peña Alhama (2)** continue straight ahead along the narrow path and past a **casita (3)** with a new roof. Turn left here uphill alternately on dirt and scree paths fairly steeply through rosemary, dwarf fan palms and cistus, also orchids and asphodel (*Asphodelus albus*) in spring. Just under 500m from the *casita* look left for some green waymarkers (**4**; the easier path; the cairns ahead mark a now eroded path) which guide you uphill.

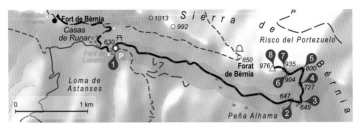

After descending a short section of scree keep to the left over difficult terrain caused by a landslip to find a narrow path to the right which traverses the hillside. You come past a cairn to a conspicuous **boulder (5)** with two cairns. Turn left uphill just beforehand (red dots) heading towards a slight dip in the ridge. Keep looking ahead for the next cairn as you ascend an indistinct path. After a tiring climb you eventually come to a broad groove where easy rock steps bring you up to the top. As you approach the top of the groove, ascend the narrow **ramp (6)** which cuts back to the right (make a note of this point for your descent).

Scramble over the crest of the ridge and head up left to a col. Scramble up to the right and behind a **rock pinnacle (7)**. Continue to the left behind it and over an exposed stretch of rock

The sheer rockface of the Bèrnia's eastern summit.

to a viewpoint with staggering views down to the coast. The rest of the route now leads onto the back of the mountain (only for experienced mountain walkers, see Grade) and across up-ended slabs of limestone to the east summit of the **Sierra de Bèrnia (8)**. Two bolts with a karabiner have been placed just beyond the summit for a climber's abseil down into a gully (start of the ridge traverse, for mountain climbers only).

Return to the **pinnacle (7**; detour: instead of heading for the descent path, keep left down to a natural rock arch), descend to the ramp and down the groove to the path at the bottom (your ascent path is not obvious from the top, but be careful not be tempted down the scree path going off to the right). Turn right and return to the *casita* and past the spring and water trough (not visible on the ascent) along the leisurely forest track back to **Font de Labarca (1)**.

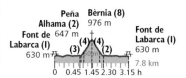

Varied round walk with spectacular views of the coast and the mountains

The impressive Sierra de Oltà (photo p. 62) is easily accessible from the coast. This walk starts along broad forest tracks and with wonderful views of the coast continues along a balcony path round the south side of the mountain before heading northwards revealing views of the mountains inland. The return route follows an attractive and interesting path back down to the starting point. Walkers preferring something more challenging can make the ascent onto the northern summit.

Starting point: Acampada Oltà, 243m. Coming from the north on the N-332, turn right at 'Calp/Calpe sur' (signpost 'Estación') and drive 2km up to the barbecue site and campsite; park here. (If coming from the south on the N-332, there's no left turn at 'Calpe sur', so go right, all the way round the roundabout back towards the N-332, under the bridge and then left.)
Height difference: 240m.
Grade: wide track most of the way, yellow and white waymarked paths, narrow zigzag path on the NE side of the mountain, then forest paths back down to starting point.
Map: IGN-CNIG 848-II.
Food/accommodation: at the coast; Acampada Oltà with limited facilities. Permission from the town hall (*Ayuntamiento*) needed for use of the campsite. Apply 1 week in advance, email: msoler@ajcalp.es, tel.: 965 874 544.
Worth seeing: Peñón de Ifach, 327m (Walk 16).
Alternative: ascent of north summit: as-

Leave the **barbecue and campsite (1)** on your right and walk up along a narrow path through bushes following the waymarkers. At the broad forest path turn left and continue gently uphill round bends and past the turn-off signposted 'La Canal, Oltà nord' (**2**; your descent

cend the Barranco de la Muela (6) to a large derelict *finca*. Before the house follow the path on the left to reach the pre-summit of Oltà and continue on the west side of the mountain to the main summit. Return to the *finca* (go left at fork) and turn left up onto the plateau. Cross the plateau to the right southeastwards to a gully. Descend in about 15 mins. to a wider path. Turn right, then left to the Ermita de Vella (4) and return to the starting point.
Remarks: the warnings of poisonous bait (*veneno*) for dogs along the route must, unfortunately, be taken seriously and dogs should be kept on a lead.

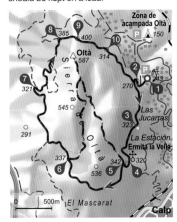

View of the Peñón de Ifach at Calp.

path). Walk steeply uphill past a spring, a chain and another **spring (3)** with views of the Peñón de Ifach emerging on your left. Ignore tracks turning off to the left and at a fork (info board) turn uphill to the right. After about 30 mins. from the start you come to a beautiful picnic area at the **Ermita la Vella (4**; toilets). Continue up the steadily ascending forest track. Ignore a turn-off right (**5**; the descent path from the summit; see Alternative) and the path bends round to the west. The Sierra de Bèrnia rises on the opposite side of the valley and the Puig Campana comes into view in the southwest. The scenery changes from luxuriant forest to a typically dry Mediterranean vegetation. Continue northwards along the path past the signpost for the 'Cim d'Oltà' (**6**; see Alternative) up the Barranco de la Muela (also Mola). Continue gently up and down along the broad track to a three-way **junction (7)**. Turn sharp right steeply uphill. As you pass the ruin of Finca Pastor you can see a pinnacle up ahead. At the **pinnacle (8)** turn right along a narrower red dirt path which leads uphill to a cairn on a **col (9**; Pas de la Canal). A pleasant shady picnic spot can be found on the right under pine trees.

Now the descent begins down a zigzag path over loose stones to reach a pine forest. The more comfortable path over pine needles continues across the hillside and down to a broad track.

Turn right (**10**). On a left hand bend take the narrower path that goes off to the right and descends to meet your original path. Turn left round two bends being careful not to miss the path off to the right back to the **barbecue and campsite (1)**.

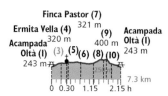

Onto the summit of a famous landmark on the Costa Blanca

Described by the Spanish writer, Gabriel Miró, as 'a symbol of grandeur, of unaproachable majesty', the Peñón de Ifach (in Valencian Penyal d'Ifac) is a towering limestone rock, rising 332 metres from the sea and 1km long, and is only connected to the mainland by a narrow isthmus (see photo on p. 59). From the top you are rewarded with a breathtaking panorama of the coast and the mountains inland. It was declared a natural park in 1987.

Starting point: Calp, car park before the entrance to the Parque Natural del Peñón (Penyal) de Ifach, 30m; from the N-332 take the 'Calp/Calpe nord' exit, carry straight on to the signpost for the Peñón.

Height difference: 340 m.

Grade: moderate walk, but at times with exposure. The limestone rocks are well worn, polished and slippery in places, especially in the dark tunnel, but difficult sections are protected with rope cables. The last part of the route requires some clambering over rocks to reach the airy summit area where a head for heights is an advantage.

Map: IGN-CNIG 848-II.

Food/accommodation: in Calp.

Worth seeing: 1. The information centre in the natural park (interesting exhibition about its abundant flora and fauna). 2. Las Salinas de Calp (former Roman saltworks, between the Peñón and the centre, provides an important habitat for numerous migratory birds such as flamingos and herons.

Remarks: 1. Limited access in Easter week and 15 July to 31 Aug. due to great crowds of people. Long waiting times possible. 2. Take a torch for the roughly 100m long tunnel. 3. The south and north rock faces of the

Peñón are climbing areas with restricted periods for the protection of nesting birds. Information on this and climbing routes in Rockfax, www.rockfax.com.

Tip: The coastal path between Calp and the Cala de la Fustera: from the car park

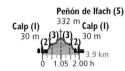

Peñón de Ifach (5)
332 m
Calp (I)   Calp (I)
30 m   30 m
(3)(3)
2   2
3.9 km
0   1.05 2.00 h

continue northwards towards Playa Levante (also Playa de la Fossa); ascend the promenade at the end of the beach and when this ends, walk uphill to the right. At a signposted turning continue right to Les Bassetes. A beautifully made path leads past delightful bays to Restaurante Timón in the tiny harbour of Les Bassetes. Continue uphill and after about 30m turn right along the coastal path to the Cala de la Fustera with *chiringuito* (beach bar, open air cinema in summer) and even further towards the next bay.

From the **car park (1)** walk up the approach road into the *Parc Natural* and in 5 mins. to the **information centre** (**2**; *Aula de la Naturaleza* and *Centro de Visitantes*). Walk up between the buildings, through the turnstile and ascend the long, shady and well made zigzag path. (Be careful not to hit your head on a tree trunk across the path half way up!). After just under half an hour from the turnstile you reach the **tunnel (3)** from where you have good views back across the harbour and Calpe's two beaches.

Walk over smooth and at times slippery rocks (rope cables) through the tunnel and continue on the other side of the mountain where the ground falls away quite steeply. The rocky path is at times exposed, but protected where necessary with a rope cable. A ¼ hr. from the tunnel turn right at a fork up a steeper path (**4**; straight on goes to a viewpoint in a few minutes). Some short sections require the use of your hands (rope cables here too). Yellow-legged gulls noisily protect their nests beside the path in May. A spectacular view awaits you at the top of the **Peñón de Ifach (5)**. Do not be surprised to meet climbers as they reach the top of their route from the south side! The views extend from Moraira to Calpe. Return the same way.

The ascent is challenging in places, but rope cables provide support where needed.

Short circular walk starting below the climbing crags of Toix west and up to a superbly located castle ruin

Morro de Toix lies southeast of the Mascarat gorge that separates it from the Bèrnia ridge. The southwest rock face is popular with climbers from all over Europe. It stands in full sun all day long and offers wonderful views across the sea. This walk leads up below the climbing crags, then along the southern slope and round the eastern tip to a residential area overlooking the bay of Calpe to eventually reach the ruins of a Moorish castle in a stunning position.

Starting point: Coming from the south along the N-332 Altea – Calp, about 500m after the Mascarat gorge and the tunnels turn right on a left hand bend into the urbanisation of Maryvilla and follow the sign for 'Castellet de Calp' uphill; park at the end of the tarmac, 175m.
Height difference: 210m.
Grade: strenuous rocky ascent at first to the masts, easy descent on the north side, then exposed climb to the castle ruin, protected with rope.

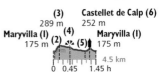

Map: IGN-CNIG 848-II.
Food/accommodation: in Calp; Acampada Oltà (see Walk 15).
Worth seeing: the dramatic Mascarat gorge (climbing routes).

From the end of the **tarmac (1)** descend the path and turn left up the steep **access path (2)** to the popular climbing crags. Keep to the left at first to avoid a rockslip, then start the steep climb up the rocks in the gully to the

View of the Sierra de Oltà from Toix.

right. There is an occasional cairn, but the route is in most cases quite obvious as it zigzags uphill. There are wonderful views across the sea as you quickly gain height. Pass the climbing crags of Toix TV on the left, an orange-coloured bowl, and keep heading in the direction of the antennae on the summit. Halfway up you see some yellow dots that are waymarkers for the route down to the beach from the top ('*placa*' written on a stone).

When you reach the top walk straight on (southeast) directly below the **masts (3)** along the unsur-

Brilliantly blue skies in February on the Morro de Toix.

faced road and 10 mins. later ignore a track off left up to the jumping-off point for paragliders. Carry straight on and round the headland of the Morro de Toix (handrail) to a **mirador (4)** where the Peñón de Ifach comes into view at Calp. Descend the roadway and arrive at the first houses in the Maryvilla residential area. Continue downhill at each junction until you see the sign for the 'Castellet de Calp'; turn left here uphill.

At the top turn right at the **signpost (5)** for the 'Castellet de Calp' and descend the path. Very soon take a narrow path down to the right into a dip, then continue sharp left and uphill to a tarmac road. Turn right to the end of the road and carry straight on along the narrow path which later veers sharp left up to a signpost. At this point you start the climb up the rocks, protected with a fixed rope, to the small castle ruin of the **Castellet de Calp (6)** with fantastic views of the Barranco del Mascarat and the urbanisation of Pueblo Mascarat. Return the same way and when you arrive at the road turn right to the **starting point (1)**.

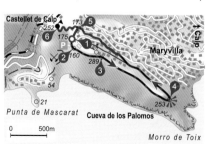

Walk up to a spectacular cliff edge

The 'ice mountain', a 6km long mountain ridge between Albir and Benidorm, owes its name to the cliffs which resemble snow in the moonlight. It offers the most spectacular ridge walk in the region – the over 400m high cliffs are among the highest in the eastcoast of Spain. This route ascends steeply to the northern summit with fabulous views across the bay of Albir and the mountains inland. The Sierra Helada (Val. Serra Gelada) was declared a natural park in 2005.

Starting point: car park, 51m, above the southern end of Playa del Albir. From the N-332 follow the sign to the 'Playa del Albir', take the first road right from the roundabout and carry straight on following signs to the Parc Natural de la Serra Gelada. After a good 500m, just after Hotel Estrella, turn right, immediately left (Carrer d'Andròmeda), then round to the right up Camí Vell del Far to the car park on some waste ground.

Height difference: 420m.

Grade: steep path, well waymarked, to the antennae.

Map: IGN-CNIG 848-III.

Food/accommodation: in Albir (promenade with cafés and restaurants).

Worth seeing: 1. Leisurely stroll to the lighthouse: 2km from the car park past an abandoned ochre mine (about 1½–2 hrs. there and back). 2. The pretty old town of Altea situated on a hill (quaint shops; church with blue and white tiled dome, a landmark on the Costa Blanca) and Altea harbour area with many restaurants and bars.

Alternatives: 1. Return the same way from the antennae to avoid a half hour steep descent on the road and walking through an urbanisation at the bottom. 2. From the summit walk along the ridge to Benidorm (black walk, Walk 19 in reverse); a good 2½–3 hrs. plus ½ hr. down into town. From there take a taxi or No. 10 bus (Benidorm – Altea) to Albir.

From the **car park (1)** walk along the signposted path past picnic tables on your left. Just afterwards ascend the steps up to the right (straight on to the lighthouse) and turn second left along a path edged with stones **(2)**. It's a steep ascent over rock through a light pine forest until you reach a level platform **(3)** with a wonderful view of Cabeçó d'Or, the Sierra Cortina, Puig Campana, Monte Ponoig and the Bèrnia. Below on the right you can see the densely populated area of Albir. About ½ hr. after the start of the walk you come to a small pine grove; continue along the edge of a deep ravine up the steep path covered in loose stones. The main path veers sharply to the right

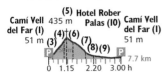

(4) before the crest of the ridge, then contours round below the transmitters and uphill to the concrete road **(5;** several paths also lead directly up to the antennae, then across a very exposed section between the fence and the cliff edge to reach the

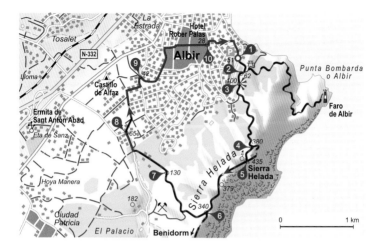

concrete road). Follow the road downhill past the turn-off for the ridge walk to Benidorm (**6**; see Alternative 2). Continue steeply downhill past a quarry and after a good 30 mins. from the summit you come to a green **metal gate (7)** which you pass on its right hand side. A few minutes later you come past some riding stables. At a T-junction turn right and at the bottom turn right along **Carrer Gafarró (8)**. Follow the road round to the left to a junction; go left and at the bottom right onto **Carrer Mitra (9)**. Go left at the end and right onto Carrer Galatea which becomes Avda. Sant Marc. Carry straight on to another T-junction. Go right here, then left and right again into Carrer Jupiter. Pass the **Rober Palas hotel (10)** and turn left, right and right again along Carrer Neptú to the **car park (1)**. (For bars/restaurants keep left down to the main road after the Rober Palas Hotel. For the beach turn right along the main road; just before the beach follow the sign 'Faro' to the right to return to your starting point.)

View across the lighthouse of Albir towards the Peñón de Ifach.

From Benidorm across the cliffs of the Sierra Helada

3.15 hrs.

Fabulous walk along a spectacularly steep coastline

Many holidaymakers associate Benidorm with skyscrapers, hoards of tourists and noisy traffic. This walk across the sheer, in places over 400m cliffs above the sea takes you away from the hustle and bustle of Europe's largest holiday destination. Along the way you are afforded stunning sea views.

Starting point: at the end of the road below the cross on El Mendívil, 220m, high above Benidorm. At the far eastern end of Playa Levante (Rincón de Loix) go steeply up a narrow one-way road to the left (signposted 'Serra Gelada' at first, then 'Sierra Dorada') and halfway up the hill turn back sharp left into Calle Sierra Dorada (straight on to the tower on Punta de la Escaleta, a breathtaking viewpoint on the cliff edge; ½ hr. there and back on foot). At the roundabout keep right and continue round bends up the road which comes to an abrupt end after a right hand bend at the top.

Height difference: 390m in ascent, 560m in descent.

Grade: strenuous walk with 4 steep, stony gullies, some scrambling on the ascent from the penultimate gully, vertiginous path close to the edge in places, PR-CV waymarkers.

Map: IGN-CNIG 848-III.

Food/accommodation: in Benidorm and Albir.

Worth seeing: the bay of Albir, lovely promenade, good choice of bars/restaurants, pebble beach with views of the Peñon de Ifach and the Sierra de Bèrnia.

Tip: if you are returning by bus to Benidorm it's better to leave your car down in Benidorm and walk up to El Mendívil at the start.

From the end of the road **(1)** go right up the steps to the cross on **El Mendívil (2)** and look down on the antennae of Radio Benidorm, the Punta de la Escaleta and the skyscrapers of Benidorm. Return to the main path and follow it to the right. Go left at the fork and descend left again at another fork down the right hand side of a small *barranco* (rock can be wet and slippery in the shade in winter), then cross the shallow gorge to the left. The path continues steeply up behind a pine tree and quickly gains height (waymarked with red arrows and dots). On your left you now have clear views across Benidorm in the south and Puig Campana inland. Follow the stepped limestone rock uphill and a good ½ hr. from the cross past two large cairns you arrive at the cairn marking the **south summit (3)**; views from here of the Sierra de Bèrnia in the north. Carry straight on along the easy, level path at the edge of the cliff (be careful not to stray too far from the path where the cliff drops vertically down to the sea). A few minutes later where the rocky path starts to descend steeply again you

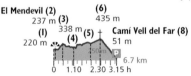

reach a beautiful, but rather overgrown viewing **platform (4)** on the right with natural seats at the edge of the cliff – a wonderful picnic spot with views of Peñas del Arabí island below (marked on some maps as Isla Mitja-

na). You can see the PR-CV marked path as it continues up the opposite side and across the Sierra towards Albir and the antennae on the northern summit come into view in the distance. Now descend the steep gully keeping away from the sheer edge of the cliffs and follow the narrow path as it ascends again. There are three more gullies like this one, the fourth one requiring the use of your hands on the uphill scramble, until finally you reach the concrete **service road (5)** which leads to the **antennae (6)**. Turn left just beforehand to follow the winding path downhill through the trees (or on the right past the antennae; very exposed) and descend the well worn path down through the pine trees. Almost at the bottom turn right at a **T-junction (7)** to meet the broad path leading to the lighthouse (1½–2 hrs. there and back). Turn left past picnic tables to the **car park (8)**. The Camí Vell del Far starts here to descend to the beach promenade. Turn left there to find the no. 10 bus (or taxi) back to Benidorm.

Along the steep cliffs of the Sierra Helada.

2.00 hrs.

Short walk with surprising views

The Sierra Cortina is not a particularly striking mountain, but it is situated close to the coast and offers a lovely walk along its broad ridge with wonderful views of the coast as far as the Peñón de Ifach in the north and Alicante in the south. It also provides a geographical perspective of the contrasting landscape of the area – the ever-increasing building developments on the coast and the unspoilt mountain scenery inland.

Starting point: the deserted La Terreta campsite, 340m, on the CV-758; after the 4km stone, coming from Finestrat, turn first right (possibly old camping sign) and park on an area of rough ground after a small crossroads.

Height difference: 230m.

Grade: comfortable walk mostly on broad paths with some short steep ascents on loose stones halfway along the ridge.

Map: IGN-CNIG 848-III.

Food/accommodation: plenty of bars/ restaurants in Finestrat. Hotel/restaurant La Plantación (www.laplantacion.com)

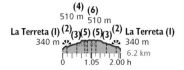

just outside the village.

Worth seeing: the 'hanging' village of Finestrat with its narrow streets and pretty houses; medieval market in May. Fiesta at the end of August.

Alternative: from the col turn left up onto the prow with viewpoint, 439m (loose, rocky path, ½ hr. there and back).

From the **car park (1)** it's a short walk up the broad track to the **col (2)** where a surprising panorama awaits you: the whole of the coastline between Calp and Alicante with the huge complex of Terra Mítica theme park lying at your feet. Turn right along the ridge. An array of flowers can be seen along the path in April and May – the delicate Montpelier cistus, mallow, asphodel, Friar's cowl, iris and globularia. After walking for about 20 mins. with two quite steep inclines take the left hand narrow path at a **fork (3**; the right hand one goes over a hill, but the two paths meet up again later on). Continue straight ahead, up a short, but steep rocky incline and soon afterwards go left at another **fork (4**;

View inland: on the right Puig Campana with the notch in its left hand summit, to the left of it the jagged ridge of the Castellets and the Peña de Sella, the Sierra de Aitana beyond.

right goes a short way uphill to the Alto de Cortina). Eventually you come to a **cairn** (**5**; a narrow, at first indistinct path leads very steeply down left into the Cortina urbanisation to meet the CV-767 to La Marina shopping centre (*Centro Comercial*) near Benidorm; roughly ½ hr. to the road; frequent bus service to Benidorm). Continue along the ridge with a wonderful view of the 1408m high Puig Campana on your right, the jagged profile of the Castellets ridge, the Peña de Sella and the summit of the Sierra de Aitana beyond with its antennae (1558m), the highest mountain in Alicante. A few minutes later you come to a second smaller cairn and, suddenly, the end of the ridge (**6**). Walk back the same way, or take the left fork at the two junctions, and enjoy the views from a different perspective.

The wonderful view from the Sierra Cortina: the end of the Sierra de Bèrnia on the left, the Peñón de Ifach in the middle and to the right, the Sierra Helada.

Wonderful coastal and cliff walk near Benidorm

This is a beautiful coastal walk from the port of La Vila Joiosa/Villajoyosa northwards to the beach of La Cala near Benidorm. The walk takes you along cliff tops with magnificent sea views and finally ascends a steep path up to the Torre del Aguiló, a defensive tower built in the 16th century, above the bay of La Cala. The descent brings you to the small town beach with a good choice of restaurants (the weekly street market is worth visiting on Tuesdays). This linear walk can also be started from La Cala.

Starting point: car park at the port of La Vila Joiosa (Villajoyosa). From the N-332 going south from Benidorm turn left at some traffic lights to the *Puerto*. Follow the road round to the right (one way) and at the small roundabout at the bottom continue straight on to the car park.
Height difference: 330m.
Grade: moderate walk with some short easy ascents and descents. Gradual ascent to the tower, but it's a steep and slippery descent, in places close to the cliff edge.
Maps: IGN-CNIG 847-IV/848-III.
Food/accommodation: in La Vila Joiosa; a beach bar (*chiringuito*) in summer on the Playa de Torres; in La Cala (e.g. Casa Modesto, an excellent fish restaurant on the beach).
Tip: sturdy walking shoes and surefootedness are an absolute must for the descent from the tower and, if possible, walking poles.

From the car park by the harbour at **La Vila Joiosa (1)** follow the path left going close to the sea. At Varadero beach walk across the boardwalk and then continue along the paved path on the other side. Just before it ends turn left up some steep steps. (Depending on the roughness of the sea at this point, you can scramble across large stones and boulders to the Playa de Torres.) At the top turn immediately right and follow a dirt path round the left hand side of a house and at the end of this (blue and yellow pilgrim shell on a post) turn right towards the rock (**2**; another pilgrim shell) and clamber up the rock. At the top carry straight on and the path bends round to the left to eventually meet a made path at the edge of the cliff in front of three blocks of flats. At the end of the path turn right and descend a stepped path to the **Playa de Torres**. Walk along the paved promenade to the other side of the beach where another stepped path ascends with a handrail (**3**; *Sender de la Costa*, coastal path). At the top follow the narrower beaten path which zigzags up the rocks. Having reached the top continue left along the top of the cliff, at first down some rock steps, then along a broad path with fabulous sea views. At a **fork** (**4**; signpost) turn left uphill towards an-

La Vila Joiosa (I) 2 m — Playa de Torres (3) — Torre del Aguiló (5) 149 m — (3) — La Vila Joiosa (I) 2 m

(2) (4) (6) (7)(4) (2) 11.5 km

0   0.35   1.30 2.00   3.00 3.30 h

other signpost and carry straight on. The path now contours round a valley. The path ascends on the other side to a tarmac road. Walk straight across the road (access down to the right to a small rocky bay, Racó del Conill, nudist beach and snorkelling area) and follow the path which ascends to a col. Descend a short way to a junction with a broad path. Turn right here and follow the path gently uphill past picnic benches to the **Torre de Aguiló (5)** from where you are afforded breathtaking views. Past the tower follow a steep and at times slippery path downhill as close to the cliff edge as you choose (or, for an easier route, descend the way you came back to

View of the island, the Peñas del Arabi.

the junction and follow the return path in reverse: turn right down the narrow path through the trees; at the bottom turn right along a broader path and later a red-paved roadway which brings you down to the beach of La Cala). At the bottom of the steep descent turn right down the red-paved roadway to the road which you follow to the right to **La Cala beach (6)**.

Return the same way to the red-paved road and straight on past the the turn-off to the tower along the signposted roadway ('Collada de la Costa') to another **signpost (7)** where you turn left uphill. At a fork bear left again uphill which brings you to a broad path at the top and straight across to the path you came on from La Vila Joiosa. Return the same way to your **starting point (1)**.

Ringing the bell of the Puig Campana

The mighty Puig Campana (campana = bell), second highest mountain in Alicante, is a stunning landmark on the Costa Blanca. It is easily recognisable by the striking notch in one of its peaks, Pic Prim, while the higher summit, Pic Gros, is more rounded. Its southern face attracts climbers from all over Europe. A steep and laborious scree slope leads up the south side (Alternative) to the summit, but the walk described here is a varied and at first more leisurely route to the top via the Coll del Pouet. The return brings you down across the south face with commanding views of the coastline.

Starting point: Font del Molí, 350m, in Finestrat. From Benidorm along the CV-758 to Finestrat and at the crossroads in the centre turn right to Font del Molí. Car park, info board, drinking water, WC and picnic area.

Height difference: 1090m.

Grade: Demanding and strenuous walk, ascent to the summit on an initially well-constructed path which later zigzags steeply over scree with areas of landslip in places; over 6km descent down a mostly loose and rocky path on the southeast side of the Puig; yellow and white waymarkers (PR-CV 289 Volta al Puig Campana) and/or cairns throughout.

Maps: IGN-CNIG 847-II/847-IV and 848-I.

Food/accommodation: bars and restaurants in Finestrat. Orange House in Finestrat: casa rural, camping, www.theorangehouse.net.

Worth seeing: Finestrat (see Walk 20).

Alternatives: 1. Ascent on the south side and descent on the north side: this route, also known as the 'vertical kilometre', is only suitable for fit and surefooted mountain walkers. It is only 4km from the start to the summit but there are 1060 metres of ascent

to overcome. Just after the bridge with the PR-CV 14 waymarker (yellow and white) keep straight ahead (left the PR-CV 289). At first a gentle ascent for about 1km to the foot of the mountain, from there almost vertically up next to the scree slope on a maze of well trodden paths; watch out for waymarkers and generally keep on the right of the scree slope, over loose stones in places where the use of your hands is also necessary. With increasing height you are afforded stunning views of the coast. At the top on the col you join the main route onto the summit. Depending on fitness allow 3–4 hrs. to the summit. Descend northwards to the Coll de Pouet and from there follow the main route in reverse to Finestrat. 2. For a shorter walk descend to the left at Refugio Vera Catral (4) and down the road to the starting point. 3. From the Coll del Pouet descend to Finestrat as in Walk 23: over a small rocky pass to the old Sella – Finestrat road, now closed to traffic, left here, about 1½ hrs. from the col. 4. Ascent of Ponoig (see Walk 23) from the Coll de Pouet. 5. Descent to Polop via Coll del Llamp. 6. Descent to La Nucía/Polop via Taberna Margoig.

From **Font del Molí (1)** ascend the road and after the left hand bend turn right up an unsurfaced track to meet the road again. Walk across the bridge and carry straight on up the broad track which branches off the road on the right. Turn immediately left along the signposted PR-CV 289 to the Coll del Pouet (straight on PR-CV 14, see Alternative 1). After 10 mins. cross a broad

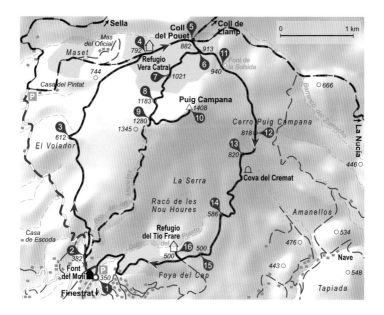

forest track and continue along the undulating path over rocky steps and scree in places. The view opens out to the left across dead trees from the forest fire in March 2006 towards the Castellets ridge, the Peña de Sella and the eye-catching pointed mountain face of the Peñón Divino with the Sierra de Aitana beyond. On you right you can see a pinnacle popular with climbers. Soon afterwards you come to a shady pine grove at **El Volador** (3; 612m). The west face of the Puig Campana then rises up steeply on your right and Roldán's notch (Tajo de Roldán) becomes visible about an hour from the start of the walk. The Puig Campana has been the subject of numer-

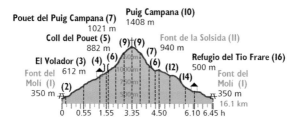

View of the Puig Campana from Sella in almond blossom time.

ous myths and legends from time immemorial. In one such legend the notch was named after the giant called Roldán whose wife was destined to die at sunset. He kicked a hole in the mountain to give her a few more precious minutes in the setting sun. The lump of rock rolled down into the sea and can be seen today just offshore from Benidorm (Isla de los Periodistas).

Eventually you arrive at the **Refugio Vera Catral (4)** on the north side of the; the hut offers shelter in bad weather (bunk beds). Leave the hut on the left and ascend steeply up to the right. The broad path steadily ascends to the **Coll del Pouet (5)** in 20 mins. (info board, signpost). A shady tree and a large flat boulder provide an excellent picnic spot. Many paths meet here (see Alternatives). Now continue up to the right at the signpost 'Cim Puig-campana' (the forest fire of Jan 2009 completely devastated this eastern side of the Puig, but regreening is quickly underway) and after a 5 minute steep climb take the turning off the main path to the right (**6**; *sender botanic*, botanical path). The path is still broad at the start, but then narrows and steeply ascends the hillside. On the way take a short detour left to the **Pouet del Puig Campana (7)**, a small snow pit. Continue uphill taking care to follow the path as it veers off right (**8**; remember this point on the return) and then zigzags uphill to finally reach the cairn on the **col (9)** in a good hour from the Coll de Pouet. Now follow the red arrows and green dots on a path which first leads you round the south side of the mountain before finally ascending to the left onto the actual summit of the **Puig Campana (10)**. Here you are rewarded with a stunning 360° panorama.

Return the same way to the **junction (6)**; turn right here. 5 mins. later you are afforded wide views of the coastline before the path swings to the right downhill, past the now dry spring, **Font de la Solsida (11; 940m)** and close beneath a vertical rock face (tiny rare rock plant in May in the crevices). Ignore several paths turning off right and left as you descend well-constructed rock steps. A good ½ hr. from the col look out for a yellow and white way-marker **(12)** leading you across an exposed section of rock on the right. The next stretch of the path offers no shade, but has wonderful views of the Sierra de Bèrnia and Peñón de Ifach in the east, the Sierra Cortina in the southeast and on a clear day, Alicante and Tabarca island in the south.

Continue on the level to the head of a **barranco (13)** and over rock slabs with the western end of the Sierra Cortina ahead of you. With Roldán's notch again on your right hand side the path zigzags down the rocks to a welcome shady spot below pine trees. Cross the top of the **Barranco del Trono (14)** directly below the notch and ascend the other side. The path now ascends rock slabs to **Foia Cac (15)** where there's a cave-house on the right. Continue past terraces to a track. Go straight across (short detour to the right to the **Refugio del Tío Frare**, **16**, an ancient stone hut (*cuco*), which indicates the former agricultural use of the land). A good ½ hr. down through the pine wood brings you to the first houses on the edge of Finestrat. At a tarmac road keep right and follow the road round a sharp left hand bend, then cross a bridge and descend in a few minutes back to **Font del Molí (1)**.

Birds' eye view of Benidorm and the Sierra Helada just to the left.

Ascent to the 'sleeping lion' and return via the highwayman's pass

This walk leads through a beautifully rocky landscape onto Monte Ponoig (Ponoch) between the Puig Campana and Sanchet. Gabriel Miró (1879–1930), the well-known Spanish writer born in Alicante who spent many summers in Polop, described the mountain as 'Léon dormido', the sleeping lion. The unmistakable silhouette can be seen most clearly from La Nucía. A very different view of the summit with its sloping terrain awaits you at the top of the mountain, as well as views of the remarkable Costa Blanca coastline.

Location: Sella, 415m.
Starting point: Xarquer valley, 700m. On the CV-770 from Vilajoyosa to Sella, drive over the bridge below the village, turn right at a group of signs on the left hand bend and continue for about 4km to the end of the tarmac. Go right at the fork, past the refugio (on the right under the trees; park here if necessary, an extra ¾ hr. walking to the start) and up the unsurfaced roadway (very uneven in places). Ignore left fork downhill after the climbing crags; continue 2km (see Wallk 24) to the PR-CV 12 signpost with barrier, then continue another 250m round to the right to park opposite a chain barrier.

Height difference: 600m.
Grade: moderate walk, mostly good mountain paths and unsurfaced tracks, waymarkers and/or cairns except over the rocky pass; some clambering up rocks to the summit.
Maps: IGN-CNIG 847-II/848-I.
Food/accommodation: in Sella (see Walk 30).
Alternative: just below the Coll de Llamp (4) turn left and follow a narrow path (3), slightly eroded in places, to Mas de la Carrasca. Turn left downhill and, as in Walk 24, back to your car (just under 2 hrs.).

From the **chain barrier (1)** walk up the forest track and round a bend at the top to the gateway for the 'Sacarest' Buddhist retreat centre (the old Mas dels Sacarest). At the **signpost (2**; straight on to Finestrat) turn up left past the house. The path narrows as you continue uphill through pine trees and abundant wild flowers in spring. When you reach a fork on a hill (several waymarkers) take the right hand path downhill. Soon afterwards a path leads off to the right (shortcut up to the col) but continue straight on past a cairn (**3**; see Alternative). At a fork turn up right (descend straight on via the Coll de Llamp to Polop along the PR-CV 13) across the rocks past a cave just above the **Coll de Llamp (4)** and rejoin the main path up to the Paso de los Bandoleros. At the top (**5**; signpost) follow the path to the left. Keep left at two

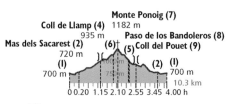

Monte Ponoig (7) 1182m
Coll de Llamp (4) 935 m
Paso de los Bandoleros (8)
Mas dels Sacarest (2) 720 m (6) (5) Coll del Pouet (9)
(I) (2) (I)
700 m 755 m 700 m
10.3 km
0 0.20 1.15 2.10 2.55 3.45 4.00 h

The 'sleeping lion' of Monte Ponoig as seen from La Nucía.

forks following the waymarkers and continue steadily uphill to where the path becomes very loose underfoot. Turn up right onto a more stable **path (6)** which joins the main path again further on (check this point for your return). The path gets steeper now as it steps up the rock towards a cairn placed high up on a rock. Soon afterwards you reach the summit of **Monte Ponoig (7)** with fabulous views of the coast (metal box and book for signatures).

Return to the **signpost (5)** on the col and to the left of the bush descend the steep rock on the easier path to the **Paso de Bandoleros (8**; rock gateway). Descend the very stony path on the other side to meet another path (left to Polop) which brings you to the right, at first over scree, then more leisurely

Soon after the start: a view of the Castellets and the Puig Campana beyond.

through the remains of charred trees (fire Jan 2009) to the **Coll del Pouet (9**; see Walk 22). Follow the narrow path on the right leading over a narrow rocky pass and down a zigzag path to meet the PR-CV 12 Sella – Finestrat. Turn right at the bottom (left to Finestrat in about an hour) and eventually you pass the signpost to the '**Sacarest' Buddhist centre (2)**. Carry straight back to the **starting point (1)**.

View northwards from the Coll de Llamp with the Sierra de Bèrnia in the background.

Through a Buddhist community onto an exciting mountain ridge

This scenically very varied walk leads through El Mundo Secreto, and onto a fabulous summit that allows a panorama of all the major peaks in the region.

Starting point: barrier below Mas el Goleró, 673m. On the CV-770 from La Vila Joiosa to Sella, drive over the bridge, turn right at a group of signs on a left hand bend and continue for about 4km to the end of the tarmac. Go right at the fork, past the refugio along a very uneven track up past the climbing crags (park here if necessary, an extra ¾ hr. walking to the start); continue for 2km along the loose, uneven track with potholes to the PR-CV 12 signpost and barrier.
Height difference: 570m.
Grade: clear forest tracks and paths at first; surefootedness and head for heights

needed in the rocky summit area, some scrambling; cairns in places, but route finding required over rockfall (Jan. 2007) and the higher sections of the ridge.
Maps: IGN-CNIG 847-II/848-I.
Food/accommodation: in Sella: Casa Roc und Pension Villa Pico (see also Walk 26).
Alternative: 1. A path cut into the rock (4) veers down to the right leading directly to the Mas de la Carrasca; about 2 hrs. shorter. 2. After Mas de la Carrasca go left at the chain and at the bottom right to the car (½ hr. longer).

Ascend the track beyond the barrier at the PR-CV 12 signpost below **Mas el Goleró (1)**. Past a path on the left up to the Pas de Goleró (see Walk 32) and further up on the right your **descent path (2)**, you come to the sign after 10 mins. 'GUHYA-LOKO, El Mundo Secreto (the secret world), Comunidad monástica buddista'. After another 30 mins. walking steadily uphill, carry straight on at a fork past the large **Mas de Papatxi** to a **helicopter pad (3**; continue straight on to 'El Salt' viewpoint over the Guadalest valley; ½ hr. there and back).
Turn right in front of the helicopter pad and then fork right along a narrower path that runs for about 1km up through trees to a col with views of the serrated Castellets ridge and Cabeçó d'Or in the south. From the

Descent from Sanchet.

Walking up to the col with views of the Buddhist community down to your right.

col keep to the right at first, then the path contours left towards a terraced bowl. Ignore a **path (4)** cut into the rock that veers down to the right and leads to the Mas de la Carrasca (visible from here, see Alternative) and continue up the narrow path through the trees. Just over 100m further on turn left up a faint path by a hunters' sign. From this point there is little or no path as you keep an eye open for the occasional cairn and head up through the trees below the rockfall on your left. Soon you are out in the open again and balancing up the rocks, finding your way as best you can in the direction of the col ahead. Look out for some mountain goats grazing on the opposite slopes. Eventually meet a red dirt path which takes you up to the col then leads across to the right to the **tree (5)** at the base of the summit block. At first up loose scree, then using your hands scramble up onto the summit of **Sanchet (6)**. From the top enjoy views of the neighbouring summit of Monte Ponoig, the north face of Puig Campana and Benidorm at the coast. (If you prefer not to climb up to the precipitous summit, turn round before the tree (5) and retrace your steps to the rocky path (4) that leads left to Mas de la Carrasca.)

Continue down the ridge past a tree just below you and after a small grove of mountain oaks zigzag back left, then right to a series of cairns down the

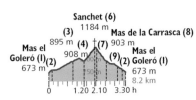

scree (7) or zigzag further left to a narrow dusty dirt path that descends through bushes. They join up further downhill. You are now looking for the continuation of the path which ascends (cairns) to some thick bushes on the left of the crest ahead. Descend loose scree on the other side until you see some more cairns guiding you across to the

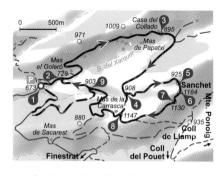

right higher up to avoid the scree. Continue down the ridge for some way balancing easily over boulders, then gradually bear left until you finally meet a narrow path coming from the Coll de Llamp (see Walk 23); turn right here to reach **Mas de la Carrasca (8)**.

Go left down the broad track. When you eventually come to a barrier there are two options: either carry straight on, then right at the T-junction at the bottom to the car (easier, but about another half an hour longer, see Alternative) or take the narrow path up to the right and follow it to a col, then downhill through trees (overgrown in places) until it eventually reaches your original route up the Buddhist valley **(2)**. Turn left here down to the **starting point (1)**.

View of Sanchet from Ponoig (see Walk 23).

Through a peaceful landscape high above the Guadalest valley

This beautiful walk runs initially through an interesting and remote landscape on the north side of the Sierra de Aitana, then continues over Peña Mulero summit and down a mountain ridge with distant views of the surrounding countryside and the coast.

Starting point: Font del Molí, 730m, picnic area. From La Nucía along the CV-70 in the direction of Guadalest, left after the 34km stone (sign 'Restaurante El Trestellador'); turn left at a group of houses after about 2km, park on the left.

Height difference: 590m.

Grade: moderate walk, ascent mostly on wide tracks, then narrow, stony paths down the ridge.

Map: IGN-CNIG 847-II.

Food/accommodation: Restaurante El Trestellador; in Benimantell.

Worth seeing: Guadalest village, in picturesque location perched high on rock above the reservoir, founded by the Moors in the 12th C; very popular tourist attraction with many craft shops, medieval castle and interesting museum).

Alternatives: 1. For a shorter more leisurely walk (grade: blue): turn left at the junction after the Corral de Senyores along the path below the ridge to the main path, 1½ hrs., almost 300m of ascent. 2. Only for experienced mountain walkers: a spectacular ridge walk to Peña Roc (do not attempt late in the day or in low cloud). Instead of descending northwest after the summit, keep straight on along the ridge as it swings round to the south towards the summit of Peña Roc. Continue along the sometimes exposed, sometimes indistinct path that runs breathtakingly close to the edge in places, but it's best to keep on the upper path as far as possible. The summit is reached after about 1¼ hrs. from the rocky cleft with some scrambling up the rocks. Return the same way. (The descent marked with red dots to the old Sella – Benimantell road through the impressive rocks of the Paso de los Contadores is dangerous and only suitable for experienced mountain walkers with good orientation skills.)

From the car park at **Font del Molí picnic area (1)** walk straight ahead up the road which soon bends to the west quite steeply. At the point where the road leads straight on, follow a **hairpin bend (2)** to the right uphill. At a concrete section carry straight on along a track (**3**; return route from the left) and about 600m further on past an old **snow pit (4**; *pozo de nieve*) on the right. Now the path ascends more steeply through a rock gateway, past the **Corral de Senyores (5)**, a *casita* surrounded by beautiful orchards, and uphill again to a **junction (6)**. Turn right here (left,

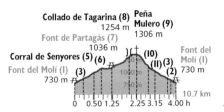

Collado de Tagarina (8) 1254 m
Peña Mulero (9) 1306 m
Font de Partagás (7) 1036 m
Corral de Senyores (5) (6)
Font del Molí (I) (3) 730 m
(10)
(II) (3)
(2) 730 m
Font del Molí (I) 730 m
10.7 km
0 0.50 1.25 2.25 3.15 4.00 h

Past almond and cherry trees below Peña Mulero (Alternative 1).

see Alternative 1) to meet the route coming down from the Sierra de Aitana (**7**; right in 5 mins. to picnic tables at Font de Partagás). After a few paces turn left again at the signpost and continue uphill (past a turn-off on the right up to a snow pit) and round a sharp right hand bend to the **Collado de**

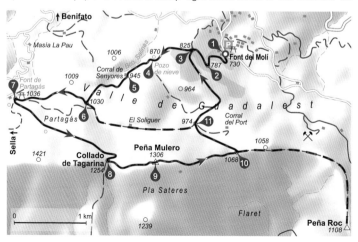

Partagás picnic area situated amongst wonderful scenery.

Tagarina (8). Turn left on the col up a narrow path in about 15 mins. to the summit of **Peña Mulero (9)** with cairn. You are afforded wonderful views on both sides of the ridge – in the south the whole of the Barranc de l'Arc, in the north the mountain ranges of Serrella and Aixorta, in the east the Sierra de Bèrnia.

Descend the tiny stone-covered path on the other side of the mountain. About ¾ hr. from the top you reach a **rocky cleft** (**10**; cairn; cairns on the right just beforehand indicate a path on the right leading down into the Barranc de l'Arc; straight on, see Alternative to Peña Roc). Descend left down a narrow path through bushes to a terrace, then continue left along the field path. This soon joins a wider **track (11)**. Turn left, then right soon afterwards onto the track which brings you back in ½ hr. to your **starting point (1)**.

Blossoming almond trees enhance the ascent to the Collado de Tagarina in February.

Wide-sweeping panorama high above the Barranc de l'Arc

The Alto de la Peña de Sella is a long undulating mountain range that provides distant views to the south. It forms the backdrop to the idyllically situated village of Sella. In contrast to Walk 30, a long, strenuous ascent onto the same ridge, this is a more leisurely walk which starts from the top end of the Tagarina valley.

Location: Sella, 420 m.
Starting point: Font Pouet Alemany, 990m, about 5km north from Sella on the CV-770, at a sharp left hand bend turn right along the tarmac road, continue about 7km uphill to the end of the valley; park at the water trough.
Height difference: 270m.
Grade: moderate walk on tracks and paths, over rocky ground in the summit areas. Marked with cairns and waymarkers throughout; exposed sections on the ridge; not advisable in low cloud.
Map: IGN-CNIG 847-II.
Food/accommodation: houses to rent in Sella (*casas rurales*) Las Casas del Ravall de Sella (www.casaroc.com) and B&B Villa Pico (www.villapico.com), both with excellent and helpful websites. Holiday

flats: Ca Isa i Toni (www.caisaitoni.com). Camping and barbecue site at Font Major (ask in the town hall in the Plaça Major); also The Orange House (www.theorangehouse.net).
Worth seeing: 1. Ermita de Santa Bárbara in Sella, built on the remains of a castle. 2. The old town of Villajoyosa (in Valencian La Vila Joiosa, the 'happy town') with colourful houses and the Valor and Clavileño chocolate factories. The famous Moors and Christians fiesta is celebrated at the end of July with the unique landing of the Moors by boat on the beach.
Alternative: just before the metal gates after Casa de Dalt turn right and in ½ hr. walk down the shady track directly to the starting point.

From **Font Pouet Alemany (1)** follow the track up to the right. Ignore an old access path to a *casita* and shortly afterwards turn left onto a rough track (cairn) that leads to a house (El Pouet). Past the house through a profusion of curry plants (*Helichrysum stoechas*), a shrub that has a conspicuously strong curry smell, the track winds uphill to some trees where it narrows to a path. Ignore the path as it continues to the right uphill and keep onto a **terrace (2)**. About halfway along you find a tiny path that ascends steeply up to the next terrace and then up two more terraces. Continue uphill through prickly bushes to the **col (3**; cairn just to the left). From the top there's a fabulous view of the Puig Campana with the Castellet ridge in front, the Amadorio reservoir and the sea. Now climb up to the right fol-

Alto de la Peña de Sella (4)
1159 m
Font Pouet
Alemany (I) (3) + (6)
990 m

Mas de Dalt (8)
1051 m
Font Pouet Alemany (I)
(9) 990 m

6.7 km

0 0.40 1.20 2.15 h

The undulating ridge of the Peña de Sella looking west from the Peñón Divino (Walk 27).

lowing the cairns onto the first summit with views now to the east of the path to the Divino and the pigeon loft on the col (see Walk 27). Walk downhill to the start of the next ascent to the **Alto de la Peña de Sella (4)** with two cairns along its ridge (a geocache is located here, see www.geocaching. com). After the second cairn descend at first left along a tiny, stony path, then over large flat limestone slabs down to the col. The path from Sella

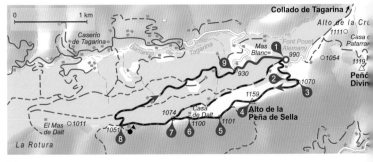

comes up to a solitary tree on the left (see Walk 30). Head straight towards a line of rock slabs going uphill and look out for yellow waymarkers. Continue up the limestone slabs and past an old fallen tree trunk on the horizon. Go past two cairns and then bear right to a **waymarker (5)** and follow the cairns, past a trig point, to the next rise where there's an old stone hunters' shelter. Now descend the path which goes diagonally right between pine trees, leads up onto a terrace and then bears left (**6**; right to the **Casa de Dalt**). Further west you can make out the house of El Mas de Dalt which was beautifully restored in 2005 and from where there was previously a launch site for paragliders. After a few minutes the path comes down to a rough track leading from the right; go left and meet another track. Go left past two large metal **gate posts** (**7**; right, see Alternative) and just under ¼ hr. later you come to a broader track where you turn right (**8**; left to **El Mas de Dalt** with fantastic viewpoint – descend a short way downhill to a rock balcony with superb view downhill to Sella) and descend in about ¾ hr. to the **tarmac road (9)**. (You could leave your car here and make the ascent of the road at the start of the walk.) Turn right uphill to your **starting point (1)** in about 15 mins.

A breathtaking view of the Puig Campana and the coast awaits you at the start of the ridge walk.

Onto a spectacular panoramic summit between Sella and the Aitana

El Divino, the divine mountain, is a very prominent mountain whose pointed summit can already be clearly seen on the drive to Sella. With its sheer south-west face it appears totally inaccessible, but this easy route from the Barranco de Tagarina approaches from the north across the back of the mountain before climbing onto its exciting summit. Legend has it that a seer lived at the foot of the Divino. People visited him to find out what the future had in store for them. They brought him gifts that are said to be still hidden in the mountain today.

Location: Sella, 420m.

Starting point: Font Pouet Alemany, 990m. About 5km north of Sella on the CV-770, at a sharp left hand bend, turn right along the tarmac road and drive about 7km uphill to the end of the valley; park at the water trough.

Height difference: 160m.

Grade: easy walk on tracks, but over rock slabs on the exposed summit marked with cairns; not advisable in low cloud.

El Divino (6)
Font Pouet Alemany (I) — 1119 m — Font Pouet Alemany (I)
990 m — (4) ┼ (4) — 990 m
1000 m
4.2 km
0   0.45 1.30 h

Map: IGN-CNIG 847-II.

Food/accommodation: see Walk 26.

Worth seeing: see Walk 26.

View down from the summit of El Divino into the Barranc de l'Arc with its terraced landscape.

From **Font Pouet Alemany (1)** carry straight on up the broad track. At a **fork (2)** make a quick detour to the right to a ruin and the Corral de Carlos, a large flat area with lovely views down into the Barranco de l'Arc – a delightful spot for a picnic. Back at the fork turn right. After about 10 mins. you reach a junction with a **barrier (3**; straight on brings you up to the Collado de Tagarina in 1 hr., see Walk 25) on the right. Pass the barrier and continue downhill past a narrow path off to the right (**4**; your return path) and you are now heading directly towards the Divino. You might be lucky enough to see a peregrine flying above the sheer rock face. The track descends leisurely, bends round to the left then ascends once more to the right. ½ hr. from the start of the walk you come to the pigeon loft at **Casa de Patarrana (5)**.

Turn right at the enormous holm oak tree and follow the path that climbs up the terraces and leads through spiny juniper bushes. The ascent

The prominent pointed summit of the Peñón Divino.

over karst limestone to the summit starts when you reach the other side of the vegetation. Look directly ahead for a small cairn on a rock that leads you right between two bushes (ignore the path to the right since it takes you along the more exposed edge of the rock). Another cairn guides you to the left round a small rocky elevation and you can ascend from here easily onto the summit of the **Peñón Divino (6)** where you are afforded a breathtaking 360° panorama.

Return the same way to Font Pouet Alemany, but just before the barrier turn left onto the narrow waymarked **path (4)** previously mentioned which brings you gently up over the hill and directly down to the Plano de Carlos. From here turn right and return to **Font Pouet Alemany (1)**.

28 *Sierra de Aitana, 1558m*

Exciting walk onto the highest mountain in the province of Alicante

The impressive Sierra de Aitana rises up in the Alicante interior and extends almost to the coast. This walk runs up along a forest track on the northern slopes of the massif past old snow pits and ascends to the summit. The descent leads past the Simas de Partagás, a maze of limestone fissures (Sp. simas), and squeezes through the adventurous rock cleft of the Pas de la Rabosa.

Starting point: Font de l'Arbre, 1172m, northwards on the CV-770 Villajoyosa – Alcoleja via Sella; just under 250m after the Puerto (Port) de Tudons a rough track turns off diagonally right (PR-CV 21 info board; drivable with an ordinary car, only very rough for the first 5 minutes, or park where you can along the track,1 hr. on foot to Font de l'Arbre).
Height difference: 500m.
Grade: broad tracks with yellow and white PR-CV waymarkers, steep rocky path and scramble onto the summit, steep descent through a rock cleft and over an area of rockfall (2011).

Map: IGN-CNIG 847-II.
Food/accommodation: in Sella and Alcoleja.
Worth seeing: 1. Four of the twelve snow pits (*pozos de nieve*) on the north side of the mountain can be seen on this walk (built at the start of the 18th c. supplying villages in the Guadalest valley and the coast with ice); 2. Aitana Safari park signposted from the CV-770 (www.safariaitana.com).
Linking tip: from Font de Forata descend to Partagás and follow Walk 34.
Tip: take extra gear – even in summer it can be quite chilly and windy on the top.

From **Font de l'Arbre (1)** barbecue and picnic aea follow the steep forest track uphill in the direction of Benifato (signpost: 11km). Look back for views of Alcoleja, Benasau and Cocentaina with its prominent castle tower on a hill. After about 30 mins. you pass the first **snow pit (2)** and after another ½ hr. you can see the domes on the summit for the first time. Go past another

pozo de nieve (3) on the left; it is usually much colder up here than on the south side and at the coast. Descend a right hand bend directly below the domes and shortly afterwards you come to a **track** joining from the left (**4**; your descent route). Continue straight ahead. Go left at a junction downhill (right in a few minutes to the third *pozo de nieve*) and a few minutes later you arrive at **Font de Forata (5**; 1374m). A fourth snowpit, 11.3m in diameter amd 6.8m deeμ, can be found straight on past the threshing circle (*era*). A narrow stony path (signpost) ascends up to the right past the water troughs which are always running with water, towards a conspicuous rock (once a shepherds' shelter). Carry straight on uphill

Water troughs at Font de Forata below the domes of the Aitana.

along a clear path directly through the pine trees. The path bends round to the right, then turns left up a very steep scree path. With a bit of scrambling you reach a point just to the east of the summit of the **Aitana (6)** with marvellous views of the Puig Campana, the Guadalest valley and the coast from Calp to Alicante. The actual summit (1558m) is a few metres to the west within the military complex. Take the narrow path leading downhill on the left in about 15 mins. to a signpost at the **Simas de Partagás (7)**; turn left along the *Sender Botànic* (botanical path) and look for some yellow and white waymarkers (part of the PR-CV 20) guiding you up the rocks to the left just above a deep fissure. As you reach the top, a lower waymarker guides you down left to the **Pas de la Rabosa (8)**. Squeeze through the narrow cleft, downclimb a short way with good hand and foot holds, cross over the rockfall and follow the slippery, stony path down to the bottom. Continue straight ahead along a lovely, gently undulating path, parallel to the mountain, that brings you back to **Font de Forata (5)**.

From here retrace your steps to the **junction (4)**. Turn right here down the track, mostly in the shade, to a left hairpin bend (**9**; follow the track to the right to see orchids in spring). Continue down the track, then go uphill again below a ruin and after a right hand bend continue for a good 1.5km along the leisurely track past cherry orchards and a house. Soon afterwards you reach a **tarmac road (10**; chain). Turn left and descend the road to **Font de l'Arbre (1)**.

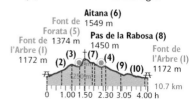

91

Walk to the highest castle in Alicante province

Benifato castle (see photo on pages 24/25; also called Confrides castle in some guides) is the only castle in the Sierra de Aitana and the highest in Alicante province. It sits perched high on a rocky promontory in a seemingly impenetrable location amidst spectacular mountain scenery in the foothills of the Aitana and can already be seen in the distance as you drive up the Guadalest valley.

Location: Benifato, 659m.
Starting point: drive west along the CV-70 from La Nucía via Guadalest and Benimantell, left after the 28km stone towards Benifato, 200m later turn sharp right up a narrow road, drive about 700m to the second tarmac turn-off, left here to a fork; park on the left before the fork (private parking opposite the newly renovated house), 790m.
Height difference: 330m.
Grade: easy walk as far as the ascent of

the castle rock where some scrambling is needed, castle area very exposed in places; indistinct red dots and arrows as waymarkers, but clear paths.
Map: IGN-CNIG 821-IV.
Food/accommodation: in Benifato Restaurante/Hostal Sant Miguel (10 rooms, tel.: 965 885 350), casa rural El Casalot (tel.: 965 666 898).
Worth seeing: 1. Village of Benifato, a settlement of Moorish origin. 2. Benimantell, famous for its olive oil (*Aceite de Oliva*).

From the **fork in the road (1)** walk uphill to the right (left goes down under a small water channel back to Benifato). Ignore a tarmac road off to the left as the road bends to the right (red dot on calvert on corner). The road gently ascends as views open out towards Serrella castle, the village of Guadalest and Benifato. Just under 10 mins. from the start a gravel track forks off to the left heading straight for Benifato castle (**2**; the PR-CV 44 Callosa d'En Sarrià – Confrides continues along the road). Carry straight on at a three way junction and follow the track as it winds uphill. After about 30 mins. you reach a wide flat area with a stone **shepherds' shelter (3)** on the right; the path continues just afterwards round to the right and zigzags uphill towards the col. When the path ends on a terrace, take the narrow path up onto the next terrace, then follow a scree path through prickly bushes to reach the **col (4)**. A few metres further left you can see a cairn marking the top of your descent route. Continue up along the

View of Confrides with the Sierra de Serrella in the background.

path to the right between two rock pillars, across a small area of rockfall, until you reach a rock arch at the foot of the castle.

It's a steep uphill climb now (in places using your hands) to the impressive castle walls of the **Castell de Benifato (5)** with views down into the Guadalest valley, the Bèrnia ridge and the coast near Calp. You can explore the remains of a tower, the castellated walls and a cistern, but be careful of a deep hole in the ground and the sheer drop on the south side. On your return do not be tempted to venture along other paths that seem to lead down the hillside from the path at the foot of the castle – they get dangerously lost amongst the bushes and have not been used in a long while. Return to the **col (4)** and follow the cairn-marked path downhill on the right (be careful in winter when the path can be very icy and slippery). You meet a broader **dirt path (6)** which you descend to the right to join a tarmac road at the bottom.

Turn right here. Leisurely descend the road to a **T-junction (7)** where you turn right again to reach your **starting point (1)** in almost 40 mins.

In order to avoid the roughly 40 minute walk on tarmac you might prefer to return the same way from the **col (4)**.

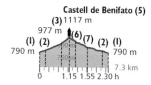

93

Very strenuous, but rewarding walk onto the mountain ridge behind Sella

The picturesque village of Sella is situated before a magnificent backdrop, the Peña de Sella, and is easily accessed from the coast. This walk crosses the rocky hillside, leads up through a steep scree gully past a deep cave to reach the impressive, undulating mountain ridge. Its gently rising and falling path crosses the ridge with distant views of the surrounding countryside before dropping steeply down back down to the village.

Starting point: Sella, 403m. From Vila-joyosa on the CV-770 to sella, cross the bridge below the village, just before entering the village turn right on a sharp left hand bend (many signs) towards the car park at the top end of the road.
Height difference: 780m.
Grade: long and very strenuous scree ascent to the cave; some scrambling to

the top; the path runs close to the edge of the ridge at times (do not attempt in low cloud), steep descent on loose, stony path; PR-CV 198 waymarkers and cairns.
Map: IGN-CNIG 847-II.
Food/accommodation: in Sella, see Walk 26.
Worth seeing: see Walk 26.
Tip: walking poles for the descent.

From the car park in **Sella (1)** follow the road uphill to the right and continue over the hill past the gates to a castellated house with garden gnomes and statues in the garden. Follow the tarmac road for about 15 mins. down the valley until you reach a signpost for the 'Ruta de l'Aigua' (**2**; SL-CV 112, green and white marked local walk which starts from the village square in Sella). Turn left here and a few metres further on turn sharp left uphill. Follow the broad stony track up the ridge through pine trees past an info board (La Solana) until you meet a tarmac road at the top about 45 mins. from the start. Turn right and a few paces later go left at the **waymarker post (3)**. On a left hand bend about 50m later on carry straight on up a narrow rocky path following the yellow and white waymarkers. The waymarkers often cannot be seen until the last minute, but keep heading straight towards the mountain until they guide you diagonally right. Eventually, after about 15 mins., the waymarkers lead to the right parallel to the *Peña*, gently up and down through esparto grass, at times across steeply sloping rock slabs (waymarker posts). After crossing three gullies with a bit of scrambling, you arrive at the foot of a **scree slope (4**; you can see a small observatory on the opposite side of the valley).

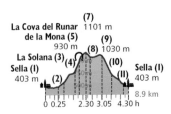

La Cova del Runar de la Mona (5) 1101 m (7)
930 m (9)
La Solana (3) (8) 1030 m
Sella (1) (4) (10) Sella (1)
403 m (11) 403 m
(2)
8.9 km
0 0.25 2.30 3.05 4.30 h

View of the Peña de Sella from below the bridge at Sella.

The ascent on the right hand side of the slope is less stony and therefore more stable. The path is unremittingly steep and takes a good ¾ hr. up to the cave **Cova del Runar de la Mona** (5; 930m; see www.geocaching.com), a beautiful and cool resting place with wonderful views of the Barranc de l'Arc. After a good rest continue uphill keeping close to the rock, and follow the waymarkers and cairns steeply uphill (some scrambling), later on to the left to find a better path **(6)**, then turn right directly up towards a conspicuous

solitary pine tree on the col (post). Turn left (right goes to Font Pouet Alemany, see Walk 26) towards a line of rock slabs going uphill past an old fallen tree. Past two **cairns (7)** keep diagonally right and follow the cairns and waymarkers to the next rise past a trig point.

Now descend the path which goes diagonally right between pine trees, up onto a terrace and then bears left (**8**; right to **Casa de Dalt**). Further west you can make out the farmhouse of El Mas de Dalt which was beautifully restored in 2005. After a few minutes the path comes down

Inquisitive mountain goats at the edge of the path on the ascent.

to a forest track from the Casa de Dalt on the right; continue left and meet another track. Go left past two large black metal gate posts and just under ¼ hr. later come to a broader track (left to the Mas de Dalt).

Cross over the track and after about 5 mins. downhill look out for a **path (9)** that goes off left at a conspicuous right hand bend (cairn; be careful not to miss this path, otherwise you will be walking away from the start of the descent to Sella). There are cairns to guide you along this path as it weaves its way downhill to a lone-standing pine tree and the start of the descent at an obvious low dark green mountain oak on the col. It's a steep path covered in loose stones, particularly after heavy rain, downhill to a single pine tree and then later a **clump of trees (10)**.

The path turns left here down to a track. Continue the descent to a transmitter mast. Follow the tarmac as it bends round to the right, then turn left onto an unmade private track and immediately left again (white arrow). A few me-

The Peña de Sella provides an imposing backdrop to the village of Sella.

tres further on descend right towards a house. Past the aptly named *Vistabella* (beautiful view) keep descending a rough path, following a power line that leads downhill until you eventually reach a surfaced track just below the chapel. At the fork descend the concrete track down to the right (**11**; a paved path goes left up to the Ermita de Santa Bárbara), round the bend at the bottom and sharp left down a path with a handrail.

At the crossroads carry straight on down some steps into the village square, past Bar Casino and Bar Paco to the end. Turn left (to the right Forn Secanet, a bakery) to return along the narrow village road to the **car park (1)**.

Easy walk through a lovely valley to the foot of a pass

This walk ascends through the delightful mountain scenery of the Barranc de l'Arc with its almond and olive trees and spectacular views. The optional detour leads up to the Paso de los Contadores, once used as a 'gate' by shepherds as they counted their sheep and goats.

Starting point: Refugio de l'Arc, 480m. On the CV-770 from Villajoyosa to Sella, across the bridge and on a left hand bend before the entrance to the village (many signs) turn right, drive just under 4km to the end of the tarmac and go right at the fork; park by the *refugio*.
Height difference: 420m.
Grade: mostly clear wide paths, steep ascent over terraces to the col; waymarkers only in the first part of the walk. Steep ascent on a very uneven track up to the col (Alternative).
Map: IGN-CNIG 847-II.

Food/accommodation: In Sella, see Walk 26.
Worth seeing: Sella and the Ermita de Santa Bárbara (see Walk 26).
Alternatives: 1. Walk up to the Paso de los Contadores, then retrace your steps to a cairn-marked path just after the first sharp right hand bend and descend left across the hillside to join the main path up to the col (a good 1 hr. longer).
2. Continue to Benimantell over the pass for lunch at Restaurante El Trestellador, return the same way (a good 6 hrs. in total).

From the **Refugio de l'Arc (1)** return to the fork (sign 'PR-CV 9 Benimantell 13km') and turn right up the forest track through pine trees (yellow and white waymarker on the first tree right). After ¼ hr. you pass a house, l'Arc del

View back down the Barranc de l'Arc from the Cases de L'Arc.

The path leads up to the Paso de los Contadores.

Canonge, on the left hand side. On the opposite side of the *barranco* there's an almost free-standing rock tower – you will eventually descend towards the other side of this rock on your return. Up ahead you can already see the Paso de los Contadores and Peña Roc to the left of it. About 30 mins. from the start you come to a group of houses, the **Cases de l'Arc (2)**.

Further up the track you pass the access track to a house, La Bodega, and at the **fork (3)** a bit later on go right. A good 1km further on just past the **Mas de Indoro** there's a cairn marking the start of a path on the left that leads up to Peña Mulera (**4**; see Walk 25). Ignore all red and blue markers on the left and right, which denote parcels of land, and finally you reach the fork, 690m, at the foot of the **Paso de los Contadores** (**5**; *coto privado de caza*; left up to the Paso, see Alternative). Continue right as the path contours almost on the level round the head of the valley with lovely views. On a left hairpin bend **(6)** turn right up a stony path that ascends at first quite steeply, then later broadens out and leads to an old **house (7)**. Leave the house

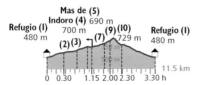

on the right and follow an overgrown path which later ascends the rock along the edge of a deep gorge as far as a spring with a water trough (now also quite overgrown). Continue uphill through the trees onto a **terrace** (**8**; the last section of path is very eroded). Follow the narrow beaten path up 11 terraces. Finally the path leads to the left to meet a broader path that comes down left from the Paso de los Contadores (**9**; see Alternative 1). Turn right as the now narrow path ascends quite steeply up through bushes to the col at the **Loma Sirventa**, 875m. Here you are rewarded with far-reaching views into the valley and beyond to Sella which you can just see in the dip between rocks in the distance.

Descend the steep and stony path between prickly bushes. Just under 15 mins. from the col you pass a gate and a sign for 'Té y Café' (follow the path to an interesting private house where you are able to get a drink some-times) and further down you come to a painted stone marker (**10**; straight on to the Pas de Goleró, see Walk 32, and towards Finestrat).

Turn right here down onto a terrace. Ascend the other side and follow the signs for Sella. Turn left at the broad track with a row of cypress trees. At the fork follow the left hand track downhill which eventually steers round towards the rock tower you saw at the start of your walk. When you eventually arrive at the climbing crags at the bottom follow the track as it bends sharply round to the left and down to the main forest track. Turn right down this track covered in loose stones below the rock faces of Tafarmaig (on the opposite side you can see the popular crags attracting climbers from all over Europe especially in winter). Eventually you arrive back at the **Refugio (1)** in another ¼ hr.

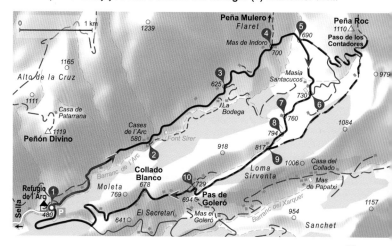

Leisurely walk with an exciting interlude

This delightful and varied walk brings you through a spectacular mountain landscape close to the village of Sella to a surprising geographical feature. The name is derived from the Valencian 'goleró' meaning funnel, which describes the narrow and steep gully down which the path descends. The second half of the walk runs leisurely down the very scenic Xarquer valley with views across to the Puig Campana and the Castellets.

Location: Sella, 420m.
Starting point: as in Walk 31 turn right in Sella at the road junction with many signs. Drive about 4km to the end of the tarmac road and fork right. With the *refugio* on your right hand side continue up along the track for about 1.5km past the climbing crags on your left. Park in the bay on the right hand side just after a turn-off left. Alternatively park by the *refugio* and walk about 20 mins. up to the start as the track is very rough in places.
Height difference: 320m.
Grade: easy except for steep descent on rocky path down the Pas de Goleró, broad forest tracks.
Map: IGN-CNIG 847-II.

Food/accommodation: see Walk 26, also www.theorangehouse.net.
Linking tip: combine with Walk 24: turn left up the broad track after the Mas el Goleró, follow Walk 24 as far as the path cut into the rock (4), turn right to the Mas de Carrasca, then continue down the broad track past two chains to the bottom and turn right to the barrier (7) in this walk.

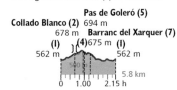

Walk a short way back downhill and follow the **track (1)** which turns off sharp right and which you passed just before parking. Continue uphill to the climbing crags and round the hairpin bend to the right. About 10 mins. further up ignore a turn-off left to the new Orange House Casa Rural.
Continue steadily uphill, round to the right at the **Collado Blanco (2)** until you eventually arrive at a house with cypress trees (3; arrow painted on oil drum pointing right towards Finestrat/Benimantell; amazingly in this location, a sign for 'té y café', not always open for service). Fork right in front of the arrow along a path that leads past the house on the right, then round a sharp right hand bend. Soon afterwards take the nar-

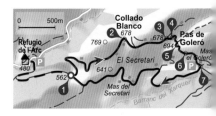

row **beaten path (4)** down to the left and across a terrace. Ascend on the far side to meet a path coming down from the left (left here to the Paso de Contadores (see Walk 31). Continue to the right slightly uphill to the top of the **Pas de Goleró (5**; it's worth making a short detour straight ahead onto the rocks with stunning views of the Puig Campana – a perfect picnic spot).

Now descend to the left down a narrow zigzag path which descends the steep funnel-shaped gully. It looks improbable, but the old mule path is well-constructed and edged with rocks. It passes a cave on the left (*santuario* painted faintly in red on the wall) as it descends over loose stones in places, especially in the lower section. Breathtaking!

At the bottom follow the narrow path through the holm oak trees and you soon reach a **fork (6)** – go left here, and left again at the next fork. The path ascends the rocks and opens out with lovely views of the striated climbing crag below and the surrounding mountains. Past a small area of construction you come to the ruins of the Mas el Goleró up on your left. Follow the path to the right down to a wide track at the bottom. Left goes up to the Buddhist valley (Walk 24), but turn right down to a **barrier (7**; signpost) and straight on along an initially steep, but later leisurely broad stony forest track high above the Barranc del Xarquer (also Charquer) with wonderful views of the surrounding mountains.

A good ½ hr. brings you back to the **starting point (1)**.

View down the Pas de Goleró.

Descent to the Barranc del Xarquer.

Short circular walk from the pretty mountain village of Sella

Sella, a pretty village in a magnificent location at the foot of the Peña de Sella, is reached along a 16km long country road that winds its way uphill through stunning scenery from the motorway near the coast. Parts of the walk take you over sections of the old Camí del Cólera (cholera path) which was used in 1910 to bypass the village during an epidemic.

Starting point: Sella, 420m. From the A-7 exit to Villajoyosa drive along the CV-770 to Sella, cross the bridge below the village, just before entering the village turn right on a sharp left hand bend (many signs) towards the car park at the top end of the road.

Height difference: 170m.

Grade: easy walk on mostly good paths, but with two short, rocky ascents; way-marked in places.

Map: IGN-CNIG 847-II.

Food/accommodation: bars and restaurants in Sella; see Walk 26. In Relleu (see Walk 36).

Alternatives: 1. Walk to Relleu: continue left uphill at the tarmac roadway and a short way further on past a left hand turning (detour to a viewpoint, 550m, with stunning views). Carry on uphill until you arrive at a signpost, 597m, indicating left down to the village of Relleu (1½ hrs. from Sella) with a good choice of restaurants (Bar Pepe in the square, closed Oct. to April). 2. Detour to the Ermita de Santa Bárbara, 487m: turn up left at the right hand bend on Carrer Valencia (7) and just before a small parking square, turn sharp left uphill. Follow the roadway round three hairpin bends until it becomes a paved path that zigzags up to the Ermita past the Stations of the Cross. At the second hairpin bend on your return take a narrow path turning off sharp left just afterwards (handrail). Carry straight on and down the steps into the Plaça Mayor.

Tip: the swimming pool is open from the end of June to the beginning of Sept.

From the **car park (1)** walk back downhill to the main road and continue up to the right and along the main road past the restaurants. Just after the last house on the left **(2)** turn left onto a steep concrete path and at the bottom turn right down to the bridge. Just beforehand a path leads steeply down to the right to the old bridge over the **Riu Sella** and back up to the main road again. Turn right here up the narrow tarmac road (yellow and white waymarker on the wall on the left after 30m).

Shortly afterwards you come to the **Lavadero de Batle** (old washhouse) where you turn right up a steep concrete path, past a house with a swimming pool with a high green fence around it. The path gets narrower as it ascends the steps of the old Camí del Cólera. About 10 mins. from the bridge you come

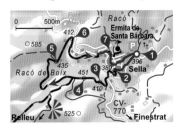

View of Sella with the Barranc de l'Arc beyond.

to a sign painted in white on the rock ahead '*Prohibido el Paso*' (**3**; no entry); turn left here away from the *Camí* up the steep rocky path at first with beautiful views into the valley on the left, then on a zigzag path up the ridge and to a broad unsurfaced track. Turn left uphill under a power line and turn right just before a left hand bend up a narrow **rocky path (4)**. Ascend this path until you arrive at a bend in a broad tarmac roadway. Do not follow the roadway uphill (the route over the Sierra del Aguilar to Relleu, see Alternative), continue down the wooded track to the right and about ½ hr. from the start of the walk the path bends round to the right uphill at the end of the valley. Soon the path joins another track coming down from the left; turn right here. With the swimming pool complex directly ahead of you continue towards a house with two large gates (**5**; Saleres de Baix). Descend an old metalled road past the house and continue steeply downhill to the bridge over the river. From here there's a detour left to the campsite and barbecue site at Font Major (beautiful spring and plunge pool amidst pink oleander; 5 mins.) Walk a few paces up from the bridge and take a tiny, steep **path (6)** that leads down to the right into the valley bottom (detour right in 1 min. across stepping stones to another pool). Walk along the left hand side of the valley close to the terrace wall past *huertas* (allotments), under a carob tree, then left up some steps and along a concrete roadway eventually to the main road. Cross over the road diagonally left and follow the sign for the 'Ermita de Santa Bárbara'. After the right hand bend (**7**; see Alternative) you come past a small supermarket on the left and Santa María bakery at the end of the road (second left) before the road bends round to the left up into the village square. Across Plaça Mayor and past Bar Casino and Bar Paco you reach a road (another baker's, Forn Secanet, just down to the right) where you turn left to return to the **car park (1)**.

103

Spectacular walk in the Sierra de Aitana

This walk in the mountains of the Marina Baixa provides unparalleled views from a stunning ridge that leads onto the highest mountain in the province, then descends a delightful path that eventually weaves back down through a vast area of rockfall to the stunningly located Font de Partagás.

Starting point: Font de Partagás, 1036m. Drive along the CV-70 from Benidorm via La Nucía to the Benifato turn-off, left here and take the second road right just before the village towards Font de Partagás (4km, quite steep in places); park at the picnic site.

Height difference: 540m.

Grade: steep ascent to Peña Alta, unsurfaced track as far as the Collado de Tagarina, then a mountain path, loose scree on the descent from the summit.

Waymarked throughout. Some exposed sections on the ridge.

Map: IGN-CNIG 847-II.

Food/accommodation: in Benifato (see Walk 29).

Worth seeing: 1. The pretty village of Benifato. 2. The Simas de Partagás (fissures). 3. The snow pit at Font de Forata.

Alternative: descent to Font de Forata through the Pas de la Rabosa: turn right at the Simas de Partagás and follow the yellow and white waymarkers (see Walk 28).

From the picnic area at **Font de Partagás (1)** turn east up a gently ascending track through almond trees – a beautiful sight in Feb/March when the trees are in full bloom (see photo on p. 24/25). About 5 mins. later ignore the first path that turns off left (to Font del Molí, see Walk 25) and carry straight on to a second signposted **turn-off** (**2**; Sella, 17km, your return path). Turn left here up the long and steady incline with views across to Malla de Llop, Serrella castle, Guadalest and the reservoir, as well as the Sierras de Aixorta and de Bèrnia. You pass a narrow path leading up right to a snow pit (*pozo de nieve*). Further uphill look back for a view of the stone archway of the snow pit. Go round a hairpin bend and after a total of 45 mins. you arrive at

the **Collado de Tagarina (3)**. From here turn right onto a very steep rocky path uphill. At the top you can see all the major peaks in the north of the province including Montgó in the northeast, Peñón de Ifach in the east, Puig Campana and Peñón Divino in the south, and Alicante too in the distance. Continue along the ridge, past a sheer drop on your right where the rocks fall almost vertically down the north side. The path divides in places, but always joins up again later. At **Peña Alta (4)** either keep high over the summit or go left through the bushes, then ascend right again to regain the main

On the descent to Font de Partagás.

path. Eventually the path descends to the **Simas de Partagás (5**; turn right to the Pas de la Rabosa, see Alternative and Walk 28). The *simas* (limestone cracks formed by the collapse of subterranean cavities) are worth exploring, but be careful of the deep sink holes in the limestone.

From the signpost continue left up the stony path towards the summit of the **Aitana**. The actual summit can be found a bit further west within the fenced military complex. Just before the fence descend to the right **(6)** down a steep gully of loose stones and a narrow winding path to **Font de Forata (7)** in about 15 mins. Turn right at the bottom onto the broader path and pass a snow pit on the left. Carry straight on at a fork and descend right at the following one. At the bottom of a steep section the now stony and slippery path suddenly narrows and zigzags downhill past a walnut tree, a spring and a water trough (**8**; **Font de Mandás**; eroded path). The dramatic, red-coloured east face of Partagás rock now comes into view. When you reach the pass, follow the path down to the right and descend through a vast area of rockfall. After a while a broader track brings you past the Sella **signpost (2)** again; continue downhill back to your **starting point (1)**.

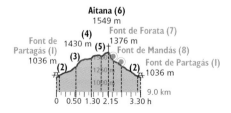

Aitana (6)
1549 m
Font de Forata (7)
Font de (4)   1376 m
Partagás (I) 1430 m (5)
1036 m   (3)   Font de Mandás (8)
(2)   1250 m   (2)   Font de Partagás (I)
1000 m   1036 m
9.0 km
0 0.50 1.30 2.15   3.30 h

To the castle high up on the Peña del Aguila, the Eagles' peak

This shortish walk includes a steep ascent to a castle high above Penàguila with stunning views, a leisurely walk back downhill through the forest and under an aquaduct from the 16/17th century with an optional visit at the end to a small historic garden.

Starting point: Penàguila, 686m. On the CV-70 from Benidorm via Guadalest and Confrides, just before Benasau turn left onto the CV-770, then right just before Alcoleja onto the CV-781. Or on the CV-770 via the Puerto de Tudons and Alcoleja. In Penàguila follow sign '*Centre Urbà*'; park near the paved path on the right.
Height difference: 340m.
Grade: steep path from the village, some scrambling up to the castle.
Map: IGN-CNIG 821-III.
Food/accommodation: in Penàguila.
Worth seeing: 1. Penàguila, of Moorish

origin, one of the oldest villages in Alicante province.
2. Jardín de Santos (Val. Jardí de Sants) before the village on the CV-781 from Alcoleja. Built in 1841 by Joaquín Rico y Soler; fountain, labyrinth, orchid house, Mediterranean trees and plants; open: see www.penaguila.es, link: El Municipio – Jardín de Santos, changes possible, often closed in winter.
Tip: visit the garden first and do the walk in the late afternoon when the surrounding mountains are bathed in a golden light at sunset during your descent.

Walk up the paved path from **Penàguila (1)**, cross over the main road from Alcoleja and ascend the steep concrete roadway to the winding road coming down from the Puerto de Tudons (CV-785). Walk a few metres along this to the left as far as a narrow, rather overgrown path which goes off diagonally right after some green entrance gates **(2)**. This path runs up beside olive trees and a little further on meets the road for a second time.

Ascend the path on the other side of the road and shortly afterwards cross the road again. Look up to see a cave, protected with iron railings, with cave paintings (*pinturas rupestres*) dating back to prehistoric times. The old now stepped path reaches the road for the last time; turn right here. Just after the 15km stone at the house of **El Coyao (3**; possible to park here for a short walk to the castle) follow a tiny path that ascends on the right of the gate up through gorse and kermes oak to a light pine forest.

The narrow path runs close to the rock and at the end of the rock face

turn up left (**4**; cairn) and follow the path to the old cistern and well on the col; from here you can look down across Penáguila to Benasau and the western end of the Sierra de Serrella; the castle ruins can already be seen to your left. Turn left towards a solitary tree and descend the path cut into the rock. Walk just below the col over to a narrow path at the foot of the castle crag. Ascend the steep path behind the castle wall to reach the ruins of a **Moorish castle (5)** with a cross (with a bit of scrambling at times).

After exploring the ruins (precipitous drop beyond to the south) return to the main road (½ hr. to the village) and walk just under 10 mins.

El Cerro Castell above Penàguila.

downhill to a sharp left hand bend where you turn right along a **path (6)**. Follow the path at first downhill, then uphill about 800m past a *casita* on the right and another casita on the col. Continue left towards a knoll and take the path just beforehand that turns sharp right **(7)** and zigzags down the slope. You come past a third *casita* with views of Serrella ridge and Benasau below it on the left. After several hairpin bends turn left at a junction **(8)** and pass a tiny *casita*. Just after crossing the **Barranco Viver (9)** be careful not to follow the path leading right towards a house, instead go left over a small embankment onto a short ascending path which joins an old forest path. Follow this rocky path steeply down to the right to Penàguila.

At the bottom, walk under a beautiful 16/17th century aqueduct before reaching the Alcoleja – Penàguila road. Cross over the road into the park and, if you are visiting the Jardín de Santos, turn sharp right down between two entrance gateposts and follow the path round the park. Otherwise continue straight on, up the steps, through the archway and left along the road. Cross the Plaça de l'Arbre, then turn left (right into the old village centre) back to your **starting point (1)**.

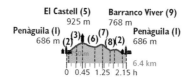

Panoramic walk over a remote mountain range beyond Relleu

A scenic drive past the ridge of the 'Sleeping Nun' just outside Relleu brings you to the starting point. The walk begins along a steeply ascending track with stunning views of the coast and the Puig Campana in the distance to reach a col at the eastern end of the Sierra de la Grana, then descends along forest paths on the north side. The route ascends once more over the wooded western end of the Sierra and returns along more leisurely paths to your starting point.

Location: Relleu, 431m.
Starting point: Barranco de los Bortolons, 780m, southwest from Relleu on the CV-775, over the bridge, turn right just after the 22km stone towards Planes and Figueretes, drive 7.2km (right at a fork) along a windy road; park at the end of the tarmac.
Height difference: 520m.
Grade: clear paths with some quite strenuous inclines.
Maps: IGN-CNIG 847-I/III.
Food/accommodation: Bars/restaurants in Relleu; Casa Rural L'Amàssera (tel.: 966 856 003, www.oldolivepress.com).
Worth seeing: 1. Relleu (pretty village of architectural interest, Moorish castle). 2. Part of this route follows the Way of St.

James from Benidorm to Santiago de Compostela. 3. Large Sunday morning market in La Torre de les Maçanes.
Alternative: 1. Short walk: at the turn-off (2) carry straight on uphill, then right after 150m. Follow the track steeply uphill until it meets another track almost at the top of the ridge. Turn left and eventually join the main path coming from the right (8); 2 hrs. in total.
2. After Mas Cortés de Dalt turn right at the barrier (7), follow the track uphill for a good 1.5km to a prominent left hand bend (just beforehand a very narrow path veers to the right downhill through the Barranc del Carrascal to La Torre de les Maçanes; forest fire in 2005; 1½ hrs. there). Just afterwards the main path joins from the left (9).

At the end of the tarmac which runs up along the edge of the **Barranco de los Bortolons (1)** turn diagonally right up the broad track (not the access road on the right). Pass a track going off left and after a good 10 mins. at a fork turn right (**2**; straight on your descent path and Alternative 1) past a pilgrim shell on a post and across the hillside with distant views of the Puig Campana, Sanchet and Ponoig. Go left at another fork past a chain barrier further on. The path bends round sharply to the left past the house, La Serra, and ascends eventually to a large cleared flat area. Follow the yellow waymarkers to the right to a col, then descend the track leading westwards down the shady north side of the Sierra de la

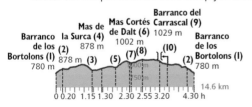

Grana. At a *casita* (**3**; Mas del Nofre) go left and continue round the head of the valley and a left hand bend uphill. ½ hr. after the col you reach the *finca* **Mas de la Surca (4)**. Shortly afterwards follow the now tarmac road as it leads more comfortably for about 1.5km to a **junction (5)** just before the CV-782.

Turn left up the forest track which later winds steeply up to a col then descends past a large farmhouse, **El Mas Cortés de Dalt (6)**. At a fork shortly afterwards go left (**7**; barrier on right, see Alternative 2 cutting out the eroded path and summit) along a narrower forest track. After another barrier ignore the track off right and continue straight on uphill. The

Autumn colours on the Sierra.

Aitana comes into view again with the Sierra de Serrella beyond. Continue to ascend a very eroded path at times for a good 1km to the top of the ridge and meet a **broader track** (**8**; Alternative 1 from left); turn right here. Walk along the open ridge just below the almost imperceptible summit of La Grana on your right with lovely views of the coastline. Then descend to a broad unsurfaced **roadway** (**9**; sign 'via pecuària'; Alternative 2 joins from the right). Turn left and after ¼ hr. turn sharp left onto a path across the terraces **(10)**. It's now roughly another 30 mins. downhill to meet your ascent path **(2)** and another 10 mins. back to the **starting point (1)**.

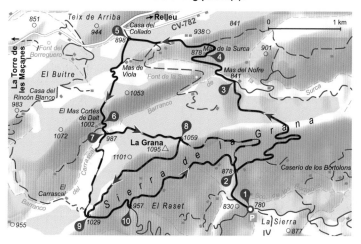

37 Cabeçó d'Or, 1209m

The summit of Cabeçó d'Or with an exceptional 360° panorama

The spectacular massif of Cabeçó d'Or (Sp. Cabezón de Oro, head of gold) towers up above Busot and is the first mountain along the coast as you drive north from Alicante. From the top you are rewarded with magnificent views of the coast and the interior. Its name comes from the rich deposits of gold once supposed to have been hidden there. On its western slopes can be found the huge limestone caves, Cuevas de Canelobre.

Location: Busot, 326m, on the CV-773, 24km north of Alicante.

Starting point: Pla de la Gralla, 521m; from Busot 4km northwards on the CV-774 until a narrow road branches off right towards the Cuevas (Coves) de Canelobre; car park on the left (info board).

Height difference: 860m.

Grade: some scrambling in the summit area; mostly waymarked paths and tracks (PR-CV 2).

Map: IGN-CNIG 847-III.

Food: at the Cuevas; Bar Ca Tona in Busot (sale of cheese and sausage as well).

Worth seeing: 1. The Cuevas de Canelobre (candelabra), with bizarrely formed stalactites and stalagmites, one of the highest vaults in Spain. Due to the wonderful acoustics concerts are held in the cathedral like interior in summer (entrance fee, open 16 Sept.–30 June: Mon–Fri 10.30-16.50, Sat/Sun/Public Holiday 10.30–17.50, 1 July–16 Sept. and Easter week: 10.30–19.30; www.cuevasdecanelobre.com). 2. La Illeta dels Banyets, archaeological site from the Bronze Age by the sea in El Campello.

Remarks: do not attempt the summit ascent in bad weather.

From **Pla de la Gralla (1)** follow the dirt track to a surfaced section that ascends steeply right. After about ¼ hr. pass below the sheer rock faces (climbing crags) on your right with a view ahead of the northern summit of the Sierra (Penya de l'Home, 1134m). Shortly afterwards you come to a small col and **Casa Gorjas (2)**. Continue downhill to meet another track (metal sign on rock); turn right. 5 mins. later, opposite the **Mas de Racó de Seva**, a narrow path turns off right (**3**; yellow and white waymarker). The well-made path, at times very steep, zigzags up the hillside with optional shortcuts. About ¼ hr. after the turn-off,

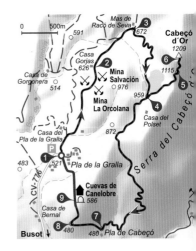

Distant views to the south from the summit of Cabeçó d'Or.

the path winds round the head of the valley, zigzags up towards the col and continues along a lovely wooded path past the terraces of the upper valley. The **summit path (4)** turns sharply left just before reaching the col. It keeps close to the rock through pine trees at first, then further up ascends a steep rock step (short easy scramble). Up through the bushes you come to a point (**5**; down left a steep scree slope) where you continue uphill to the right (remember this point for the descent!). Continue steeply up the rocks again to a rock gateway. As you start the final 10-minute ascent to the summit keep to the right at first, then turn left past a cistern to reach the summit pillar of **Cabeçó d'Or (6)**. From here you can enjoy a wonderful 360° panorama of the coast to the northeast near Calpe, Montcabrer and Els Plans to the north inland and El Maigmó with its conspicuously pointed summit in the west.

Return the same way, but when you reach the scree slope do not be tempted to continue downhill, go left instead up across the rock (**5**; waymarker). In ½ hr. you arrive at the **col** (**4**; return the same way in about an hour back to the Pla de la Gralla). Continue left to the Casa del Polset, then turn left down a lovely, but very long and twisting mountain path a good 3km to the **Pla de Cabeçó (7)**. From the valley bottom go right (signpost) and a few minutes later ascend a steep and tiring path (**8**) – a tiring climb of at least 20-minutes up to the **Cuevas de Canelobre (9)**. From here it's a leisurely walk down the road in just under 15 mins. to the **Pla de la Gralla (1)**.

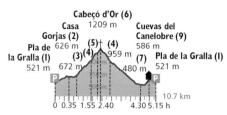

111

One of the most delightful walks on the Costa Blanca

From below, the Serra dels Plans does not seem very remarkable, but the panorama from the top offers a view of all the significant peaks in the surrounding area. The walk begins from the quiet village of La Torre de les Maçanes (Sp. Torremanzanas), leads past a well-preserved pozo de nieve (snow pit) before ascending to the panoramic summit and returning to the village over another summit and along a delightful path through remote mountain scenery.

Starting point: La Torre de les Maçanes, 793m. Casa de Cultura at the highest end of the village. Drive from Relleu on the CV-782. At the crossroads turn right, follow the road past the Torre Almohade (tower) as it bends round left to descend to a roundabout. Go right and park in a lay-by.

Height difference: 620m.

Grade: two steep ascents, waymarked throughout.

Map: IGN-CNIG 847-I.

Food/accommodation: in La Torre de les Maçanes: Hotel/Restaurant El Sester (tel.: 965 619 017, www.hotelsester.com).

Worth seeing: 1. Torre Almohade built in the time of the Almohads (Moroccan Berbers), the most significant political power in the 12/13th C). 2. The feast of Pa Beneït, celebrated since 1658 on 9 May, the festival of the Holy Bread in honour of San Gregorio who freed the village from a plague of locusts. Young women, dressed in traditional costume, process to the church carrying huge loaves, decorated with flowers, on their head to offer to the saint. 3. Typically Spanish market every Sunday morning until 1pm.

Low-lying mists and mountain silhouettes; the pointed summit of El Maigmó on the left.

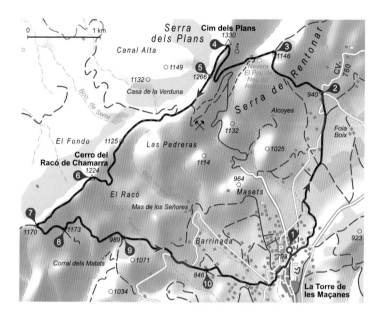

From the **lay-by (1)** return to the roundabout, go left a short way up the road to a signpost and turn left again. Carry straight on across a dry river bed, follow the path left until it ascends steeply to a track (shortcut beforehand to the right); turn right onto the track. Eventually you meet the CV-780 to Benifallim. Follow the road to the right past Font d'Obits until you come to another sign for the 'Mas dels Castellans' (**2**; you can park here if you only want to walk to the summit and back). Directly opposite at a *via pecuària* sign ascend the narrow and eroded path steeply uphill.

The path soon levels out on the right hand side of a *barranco*, then ascends again very steeply northwestwards. You can see the summit ahead of you

with an antenna and a small white building. 5 mins. later the domed roof of the snow pit comes into view. Continue up the path, around a fallen tree (the path left brings you directly up to the snow pit), and steeply uphill towards the pylon. Go below the power lines towards another pylon, but before you reach it, turn left along a path **(3)** which joins a track. Continue up left and after just under 1½ hrs. from the start you reach the *pozo de nieve*, El Pou del Rentonar, which was built at the start of the 18th century. There's a sign-post opposite the entrance to the snow pit. Ascend a rocky path which then leads northwestwards with views down left of La Torre de les Maçanes and Cabeçó d'Or. Continue steadily uphill along an old mule path. ¼ hr. from the snow pit to a junction and turn right to a second junction (PR-CV signpost; left here to (5), shortcut without summit ascent). The views open out eastwards of the Aitana and the Puig Campana. Continue uphill to the right to the **Cim dels Plans (4)** with further views of Alcoi in the north, the Barranc del Sinc to the left with Montcabrer beyond, and the summits of Migjorn and Maigmó in the southwest. Look out for sightings of an eagle. (From the summit you can continue along a surprisingly good path on the ridge to the north and in about 20 mins. come to a conspicuous rib of rock on the right and a lovely picnic spot out of the wind. With luck you might see some small mountain goats along the ridge as they spring daringly from rock to rock.)

From the summit take the broader track that descends down to the right. At a **junction (5)** continue steeply downhill a long way over loose stones before the track ascends again. It's a very steep incline up to a large mountain oak tree on the top of **Cerro del Racó de Chamarra** (**6**; cairn); descend right to regain the track and continue downhill quite a way until you come to a **sign-post (7)**; turn left along a ridge. At another **signpost (8)** turn left towards La Torre de les Maçanes. This path narrows as it contours round the hillside. Continue along the pretty path which runs at times over rock and then down-hill to the **Corral dels Matats (9)**, a cave once used as an animal pen (infor-mation board). Shortly afterwards turn left, then at the fork descend the right hand side of a *barranco*.

Just under ¼ hr. from the *Corral* you descend to a tarmac road where you turn left past a large modern building. At a left hand bend carry straight on down a track until you see a yellow and white waymarker guiding you left down a narrow **path (10)** through a furrow which leads to a tarmac road; turn right here. Take the narrow path up to the left to avoid the new red iron gates. Continue downhill until you come to a distinct right hand bend. Take the con-crete path straight on that quickly leads down to the main road. Cross over the road and go diagonally left onto a tarmac road, straight on uphill at the right hand bend and then right at the top. At an information board carry straight on to your **starting point (1)**.

Beautiful light on the terraces of the Serra dels Plans.

Beautiful gorge walk with spectacular rock scenery and griffon vultures

The Barranc del Sinc (also Cint) near Alcoi (Sp. Alcoy), with its impressive rock faces, cuts deeply into the Sierra de Mariola. This walk starts through the dramatic entrance to the gorge, leads into a leafy arbour beside the stream, then over a remote wooded hillside back down towards Alcoi with views of the mountain landscape in the east.

Starting point: Alcoi, PR-CV 57 walking sign, 676m. Drive to Alcoi on the N-340 and follow signs to Banyeres over a suspension bridge, turn left at the roundabout along the CV-796 and about 4km further on until the CV-796 turns off to the right signposted to the 'Preventori Mariola'. Continue roughly another 4km, past the Preventori (picnic area; formerly a tuberculosis sanatorium), and continue a good 1km downhill to an obvious hairpin bend (walking sign on left). Park on the left just beforehand.
Height difference: 580m.
Grade: footpaths and tracks, ¼ hr. uphill on tarmac; GR and PR-CV waymarkers. A forest fire in July 2012 has affected parts of the area after Mas de Capellá.
Map: IGN-CNIG 821-III.
Food/accommodation: in Alcoy; bar opposite the 'Preventori'.
Worth seeing: the town of Alcoi is well worth a visit with its many interesting buildings and beautiful town square, especially the Plaza de Dins. The annual Cabalgata de Reyes, procession of the Three Kings, the oldest and most famous in all of Spain, 5th January; the equally famous Moros y Cristianos fiesta at the end of April (Museo de la Fiesta, Carrer San Miguel, 1 €).
Alternative: Ascent to Montcabrer (forest fire July 2012; see Walk 40): shortly after El Mas de Capellá take signposted turn-off left up to the Coll de Sabata (also Zapata) and further to the summit (1¼ hrs. there).
Tip: 1. To vulture viewpoint (1 hr.): from the Preventori follow signs northwards to Ermita de San Cristóbal and walk about 1km further on to a point above the gorge. 2. Further walks from tourist office in Alcoi (Sant Llorenç 2), close to the Plaza de Dins. See also www.alcoiturisme. com (link: Naturaleza – Rutas verdes).

From the **walking sign (1)** go left and you immediately have a stunning view of the start of the Barranc del Sinc where it's possible to see griffon vultures all year round (see Tip). Continue up the causeway and through the narrow entrance to the gorge with beautiful caves and striations high up in the rock. Ascend some steps and shortly afterwards pass a *casita* with a vegetable garden and later on some plane trees. A shady section begins after a spring. Ascend the well-made path until you see another *casita* up on the right above. At the fork at the **Ombría de Garrofer (2)** continue to the right along the left hand side of the *barranco* with blackberry bushes in summer and rosehips in October. The path crosses over the *barranco* several times on its way to a small pumping station, then ascends steeply to a tarmac road. Turn left uphill and after about 15 mins. of steady uphill walking you reach the set-

The narrow entrance to the gorge at the start of the walk.

tlement of **Les Casetes de Vilaplana (3)** with open views to the left of wooded hills and crags. At the prominent bend in the road follow the GR route to the right (waymarker on corner of house). Just after a left hand bend the narrow red and white marked **GR-7 path (4)** turns right up through the wood, a possible shortcut to the main path further up. After a chain barrier the track sweeps round the hillside to the left and ascends a gentle incline past fruit and almond trees to the Mas de Capellá. Turn right here and pass another grove of trees on your right. The now stony track continues

uphill to the right. Ignore the clear path turning off left (ascent to Montcabrer, see Alternative). This lovely high path through a beautiful mixed wood affords views to the southwest. At a 4-way **junction (5)** ascend right and then downhill past an ivy-covered crag (just beforehand take a detour up to the right to the ruins of a castle in a panoramic location), then continue round a hairpin bend to a waymarked shortcut about 10 mins. later (**6**; or from the 4-way junction descend left, then right to this point). Descend steeply through the wood and almost at the bottom keep right along the narrow wooded path which brings you round to the picnic area of **Font de Serelles** (**7**; stone seats and tables, barbecue sites). Continue downhill (another shortcut on a left hand bend to the right down a

Dramatic rock scenery at the start of the Barranc de Sinc.

steep, narrow path) until you eventually come to a green and white marked *senda local* (**8**; local path) to the right.

Descend to the top end of a tarmac road in an unfinished urbanisation. (At the time of writing it was possible to turn right along the surfaced road and find a narrow dirt path uphill to the brickworks chimney.) However, continue downhill, find a **path (9)** along the right hand side of a small *barranco* which leads to the Font del Xorrador. Shortly before you reach the spring follow a narrow steep path uphill on the right **(10)**. Turn left to the chimney and left again back to your **starting point (1)**.

Beautiful ascent onto the highest mountain in the Sierra de Mariola

The limestone massif of the Sierra de Mariola stretches across the border between the provinces of Alicante and Valencia. It acquired natural park status in January 2002 and is renowned for the beauty of its hills although, sadly, a forest fire in July 2012 destroyed acres of land stretching about 2km north of the Coll de Sabata to the Loma de Benifleta. The Mariola is of great botanical interest with an abundance of medicinal plants and aromatic herbs, considerable stands of pine trees and scattered small forests of, amongst others, yew, maple, ash and oak. The summit of Montcabrer crowns the Sierra and affords spectacular views over the surrounding countryside.

Starting point: Ermita de Sant Cristòfol, 551m (San Cristóbal) near Cocentaina. From Alcoi on the N-340 to Cocentaina. After the turn-off to the centre turn left at the roundabout signposted to the Ermita Sant Cristòfol. Park at the picnic and barbecue area.
Height difference: 1150m.
Grade: long, steep ascent; yellow and white PR-CV 37 and red and white GR signs and waymarkers. Although much of the forest has been destroyed (July 2012) in the second half of the walk, the waymarkers have been repainted and new signs erected.
Maps: IGN-CNIG 821-I/III.
Food: in Cocentaina.

Alternative: 1. Short walk up to the Castell de Cocentaina, 749m: from the car park go up the steps opposite the information board through the *área recreativa* and to a concrete road. The road winds steeply uphill for a long way to the castle tower which is situated in a breathtaking location on the hill to the west of Cocentaina (visible for miles around). The paved footpath to the castle is exposed in places, but offers amazing views; 1½ hrs. in total. 2. Descent along the GR-7 (a good 1km shorter).
Tip: the creatively designed picnic area has cool deep caves with benches, barbecues, stone tables and seats, and toilets. There's also a restaurant, open lunch times.

Follow the narrow tarmac road that runs below the **Ermita de Sant Cristòfol (1)** to the northwest and ascends steeply to a painted, tiled info sign. The path ascends on the left with a handrail up through a pretty pine forest.
Below an overhanging rock face past a stone table and bench you then ascend steep rock steps, past another picnic table at the **Font de Penya Banyà (2)**, before the path zigzags up to the next spring. The views soon open out of the Embalse de Beniarrés. Then follows a level section to a **viewpoint (3)** where there is another map on beautiful painted tiles with the names of all the surrounding peaks. Now continue directly below the sheer rock face to the **Font Huit Piletes (4)**. Ascend the steep path going up on the left from the spring and eventually past another **viewpoint (5)** with a wooden cover. Continue uphill, past another stone table, and a while later up

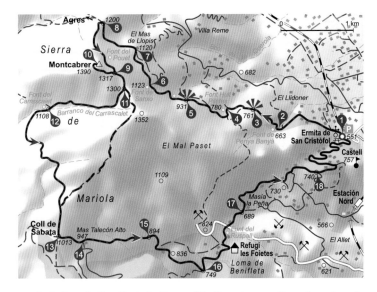

a set of steps to the **Font de Sanxo (6)**. From here walk northwestwards along a narrow path, sometimes over sloping rock, sometimes through prickly bushes. The path is protected with a handrail in exposed places.

After over 500m of ascent you are now heading gently downhill along a beautiful section of the path towards the farmstead of **El Mas de Llopis (7)** on a promontory. Walk past the house on the left and ascend the slope up to a **signpost (8)**. Straight on goes to Agres, but you turn left along the PR-CV yellow and white signposted path to Montcabrer steeply up past the **Font del Pouet** (now also with red and white GR waymarkers) to the **col (9)**. Go right here and in a few minutes you are standing on the summit of **Montcabrer (10)**.

Back at the **col (9)** follow the GR waymarkers straight ahead, past a cairn that marks the quick descent left to Font de Sanxo, to a **signpost (11)** on the far side of the col (les Monteses) The GR turns left here (Alternative), but you begin the steep descent down to the right through the Barranco del Carrascalet. A good 45 mins. from the summit you come to a **signpost (12)**; turn left towards the Coll de Sabata. After a good kilometre from the sign you come over a rise suddenly into the area of the Mariola destroyed by fire. Continue up and down along the path (past the turning where the GR rejoins your path; see Alternative) until you finally reach the **Coll de Sabata (13)** at a signpost indicating left to the Castell de Cocentaina (the GR-7 turns right here; see Walk 39). Descend left along the narrow path through pines to the ruin of a large *finca*, the **Mas Talecón Alto (14)**, and then left to continue the steep descent over rocky ground. The **path (15)** starts its long zigzag descent down the right hand side of a gorge then ascends to a broad track out of the fire area and past a *casita*. Soon you will see a quarry on the left and straight ahead the Castell de Cocentaina, your next goal.

Walk through a hunters' area on the Loma de Benifleta and descend to a roadway **(16)**; turn left. When you come to a sign indicating the Refugi Les Foietes (2 mins., toilets, sometimes open at weekends) turn left and then right soon afterwards. Continue downhill and cross over the road that leads up left to the

The castle tower high above Cocentania.

quarry onto a path. Descend to a track and turn left downhill to a signpost which indicates left to 'Castell, Sant Cristòfol' **(17)**.

Follow this path to directly beneath the impressive orange-coloured rock faces with deep indentations – a popular climbing area – where it bends to the right and leads up through a forest to eventually join a wide track. Go left here to a road and left again uphill towards two beautiful houses on the col. At the top turn right uphill along the tarmac road (ignore the path opposite which is no longer in use) and a few mins. later turn off left along another path **(18)**. The castle finally comes into view and you soon reach the concrete road that winds downhill in 20 mins. back to the starting point at the **Ermita de Sant Cristòfol (1)**.

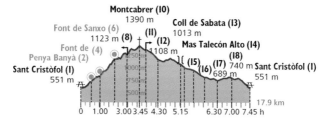

In the footsteps of the textile merchants

This walk, in the province of Valencia and the comarca of La Vall d'Albaida, takes you past several derelict, mostly overgrown mills which, with the arrival of electricity were relocated to within the town. In the 15th and 16th centuries Bocairent was a busy agricultural area and was also known for its textile production. The water from the Barranco de Ontiniente (Val. Ontinyent) was needed for the manufacture of textiles and the finished bales were transported on mules into the villages along the Camí de l'Escaleta. Due to a forest fire which raged through the gorge in 2010, the character of this walk has completely changed, but ironically, has made it more interesting and dramatic.

Starting point: Bocairent, 600m. From Alicante drive along the A-7 to Villena, then on the CV-81 towards Bocairent. At the first roundabout after the bridge into town, turn off left (after the 13km stone); turn left at a small crossroads and park on the right.

Height difference: 340m.

Grade: mostly waymarked route, start and end along the PR-CV 122. Narrow stony path through the gorge, steep ascent to Castellar.

Map: IGN-CNIG 820-II.

Food/accommodation: bars and restaurants in Bocairent, also hotels.

Worth seeing: 1. Barrio Medieval, the old town centre (descend left from the starting point, go across the bridge and follow the sign left for the Ruta Mágica which brings you up an ancient pathway to the town hall square (tourist info). 2. Les Covetes dels Moros (Sp. Cuevas de los Moros), said to

be cut into the rock in 10/11th C. in the time of the Berbers, probably for storing grain: descend from the square to the caves or carry straight on from the bridge.
Info at www.bocairent.org.

Walk back to the **crossroads (1)** and ascend the road past a cross. Shortly afterwards turn left beside a fence round some large modern houses. The Ermita del Santo Crist stands high on the hill up on your left (accessed from the town centre past the Stations of the Cross). The path descends to a **signpost** (**2**; straight on, your return route). Turn left and very soon diagonally right onto the **Camí de l'Escaleta** (stepped path), an old mule path that leads up steps cut into the rock. At the top go left at a fork, then cross a broad track to follow a narrow path which descends into the Barranc dels Tarongers (in Valencian, gorge of the oranges). The path zigzags downhill and the first old textile mill comes into view in the valley bottom. Continue to descend the right hand side of the *barranco* and about 45 mins. from the start of the walk arrive at the **Molí de Pep Joan** (**3**). Ignore a turning to the right bringing you up to the Coll de Dona and continue down the gorge past the Molí de Beneito (Casa de Beneyto), built in 1902, to the huge **Molí de Julians** (**4**) standing amidst poplars. Cross over a stream and af-

The pretty medieval town of Bocairent.

ter another turn-off right to the Alt del Castellar you reach the **Molí de Lluna (5)**. Soon afterwards pass some new buildings at the old **Molí de Patiràs (6)**, then a spring, the Font de Barranc dels Tarongers, followed by a water control building (with parking area). You finally reach the CV-81, the very busy road between Bocairent and Ontinyent. (Detour less than 1km away to the left to Pou Clar, a natural bathing pool in a beautiful rocky landscape.) Opposite you will see the climbing crag known as the Cagalló del Gegant (meaning giant's turd).

Follow the green and white marked **SLV-9 path (7)** that zigzags uphill on the right to **Alt del Castellar (8**; 654m). From the summit carry straight on (cairn) down to the **Coll de la Dona (9)**, then uphill again along the **Camí Vell (10)** which, a bit later on, leads through a cutting in the rock. About 300m after-

wards at a fork go right (yellow arrow) and at another junction turn left over the brow of a hill. Descend the hillside, turning right at the following junction, and continue all the way down to the **signpost** (**2**) and your **starting point** (**1**).

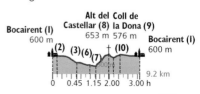

123

Circuit through an almost unspoilt landscape

The nature reserve of the Parc Natural del Carrascal de la Font Roja extends across the Sierra del Menejador (also Menechaor, Menetjador) in the municipal areas of Alcoi and Ibi. Its east-west orientation highlights the contrast between the shady northern slopes and the sunny southern hillsides offering a wonderful scenic diversity. Here you can still discover a typically Mediterranean forest area with, for example, holm oak (Sp. carrasca, bot. Quercus (ilex) rotundifolia), maple, yew and ash. The circular walk leads up through the beautiful naturally preserved mixed forest with extensive views across to the Sierra de Mariola.

Starting point: Santuario de la Font Roja, 1050m. From the N-340 south of Alcoi turn off north-westwards and drive for about 9km along the CV-797 to the Santuario (car park, picnic area).
Height difference: 340m.
Grade: mostly broad yellow marked forest tracks, well-constructed stepped path on descent past the charcoal burner site.
Map: IGN-CNIG 846-II.

Food/accommodation: Restaurante Font Roja (Tue–Sun lunchtimes); in Alcoi.
Worth seeing: visitor centre, once a hotel in 1920s, by the Font Roja sanctuary (open Tues–Sun/public hol. 9.30–14.00).
Tip: brochures about the fauna and flora of the area, snow pits, charcoal burner sites and two other walks (red, 1½ hr.; blue, ¾ hr.) available from visitors centre. Several picnic spots by the road before the Santuario.

From the car park at **Font Roja (1)** walk up the steps past the toilets, then go left past a row of old summer houses to the picnic area of La Glorieta dels Paellers (barbecues, stone tables). Continue uphill to the **Cova Gelada**, a cave with a constant temperature of 7° C. It's a gentle ascent past a **turn-off** to the left (2; your descent route), then the broad track gets steeper as it ascends for about 10 mins. to the Pla dels Galers; the red route turns off here to the right. Information boards about the flora and fauna are located at the side of the path. Sign no. 4 further on indicates right to the **Mirador de Pilatos viewpoint (3)** with a view across the whole of the park: Alcoi and Montcabrer in the northeast, in the north and northwest the broad terraces before the wooded slopes of Loma de la Fontfreda in the province of Valencia. The track now descends before going steeply uphill again and arrives at the former mountain farm of **El Mas de Tetuán (4)**. Straight on

A watering place for wild boar; Maigmó in the distance.

goes along the PR-CV 26 to Ibi (3.9km further on) and the GR 7 descends to the right after the farm to Elda, but you follow the PR-CV 26 marked track round a left hand bend towards Menejador (2.4km). After a steep incline you come to the **Cava Coloma** snow pit **(5)**, ideally situated and protected from the sun. As you reach the top of the steep incline the views open out across the wooded slopes of the Sierra de Carrasqueta towards Cabeçó d'Or and to Ibi with its factory roofs gleaming in the sun. You pass a **pool (6)** with a roof on the right for *jabalí* (wild boar).

You are now heading directly for Menejador. Just before a water tank a narrow waymarked **path (7)** turns off right and leads down past 3 snow pits, see Walk 43 (straight on a 10-minute detour to reach the summit of Menejador, 1354m, with a weather station and viewing platform from where you can enjoy beautiful views across the whole nature reserve.) Turn left downhill and after 50m descend left through the forest along a former **charcoal burners' path (8)** that zigzags steeply downhill over well-made steps and past the site of a **former kiln (9**; *carbonera*) on the right further down. At the bottom turn right onto your **outward path (2)** and return to **Font Roja (1)**.

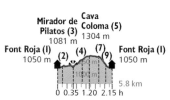

125

Round walk from Ibi with an ascent onto Menejador, 1354m

5.30 hrs.

Along the Camí dels Geladors, the ice merchants' path

Ibi, originally of Iberian origin, lies between two hills on which the hermitages of Santa Lucía and San Miguel are located (the latter said to be built on the ruins of a Moorish castle). Ibi became a pioneer of the ice trade which continued until the start of the 19th century when it expanded to incorporate the manufacture of ice-cream. However, Ibi today is known worldwide as the largest toy manufacturing centre in the country. This walk runs along the ice merchants' path on which the ice was transported down into Ibi. On the way it makes an ascent onto Menejador, returns past four snow pits and descends through a delightful gorge back to Ibi.

Starting point: Ibi, 784m. From the town hall ascend Av. Joaquín Vilanova towards the 'Parc Natural de la Font Roja'; park at the top where you can before the left hand bend (PR-CV 26 walking sign).
Height difference: 740m.
Grade: strenuous ascent to Mas de Tetuán, rocky paths in places; way-marked yellow and white throughout.
Map: IGN-CNIG 846-II.
Food/accommodation: in Ibi.
Worth seeing: 1. The old town of Ibi. 2. Museo Valenciano del Juguete (toy museum; closed in 2013 due to renovations, info: www.museojuguete.com).
3. The Festa dels Geladors (ice merchants' festival, in February).
4. Enfarinats, large flour fight on 28th Dec. (Día de los Santos Inocentes – day of the innocent children, the Spanish version of April Fools' Day).
Further info: www.ibi.es.
Alternative: from the water tank at the foot of Menejador walk down to the Santuario de la Font Roja (a good 30 mins., see Walk 42).

Walk up the road from the **car (1)** to a left hand bend. Ignore the signposted turn for the PR-CV 26 and take the next right onto a **path (2)**. Keep left and cross over a small *barranco*. Ascend steeply on the other side and come to a pylon with a waymarker. When you reach an asphalt road carry straight on and continue on the right below a small pumping station and three pines. At a cairn look out for the waymarkers leading you directly up the rock on the left **(3)**. It's a fairly steep ascent, but you gain height quickly and soon leave the views of the industrial town of Ibi behind.

After a good 30 mins. from the start of the walk, you come to a solitary pine tree where the views open out to the west. About 15 mins. after that you enter a pine forest and the atmosphere changes

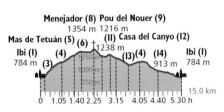

Menejador (8) Pou del Nouer (9)
1354 m 1216 m
Mas de Tetuán (5) (6) (11) Casa del Canyo (12)
Ibi (I) (4) 1238 m (13)(4) (14) Ibi (I)
784 m (3) 913 m 784 m
15.0 km
0   1.05 1.40 2.25 3.15   4.05 4.40 5.30 h

Views from Menejador towards Alcoi and the coastal mountains north of Dénia.

completely along the gently undulating path at the edge of a *barranco*. After a steeper incline you eventually reach the **Casa de Foiaderetes (4)**. You then cross over a forest road (signpost) and walk past a stone cistern and a 'Parque Natural' barrier. Later on the path leads through the pine forest again with views of the coast and the Sierra del Maigmó. Ignore all turn-offs to the left and right, and after almost 2 hours walking uphill from the start you finally reach the former farm house **Mas de Tetuán (5)** and the adjacent *era* (threshing circle; info board about an ancient yew tree which is one of only a few examples in the park. The red and white marked GR 7 path turns down left to Elda or carries straight on to Font Roja; see Walk 42).

After taking a well-earned rest turn right up the broad track on the PR-CV 26 in the direction of the 'cumbre Menejador'. The path ascends quite steeply and you pass the deep snow pit of **Cava Coloma** (**6**; also Pou de Carrascal) with an echo. The path bends to the left and shortly afterwards you pass a pool for wild boar on the right. Continue with distant views on your right until you reach a **water tank (7)** on a col. The path continues down left to Font Roja, however you ascend the path straight ahead to reach the summit of **Menejador (8)** with weather station and viewing platform (the concrete track also goes to the top) allowing extensive views of the park, the province of Valencia in the west and the mountains in Alicante province in the east.

Back at the **water tank (7)** follow the yellow and white marked ice merchants' path steeply down on the left. You are now following the snow collectors' path. Hundreds of years ago this path was used for transporting the

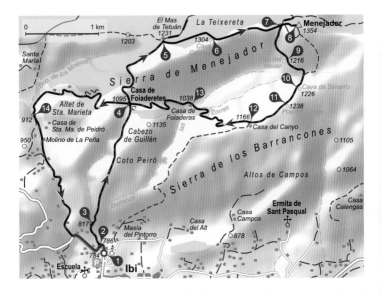

precious ice from the snow pits at night down to Ibi on the backs of mules. A few minutes later you pass an old stone well with a trough and after a short level section, you reach the large **Pou del Nouer (9)**.

Go to the left around the snow pit and descend towards the Barranco de las Zorras (also las Cimas). Descend into the gorge and continue up the opposite side to the **Cava de Simarro (10)**, the largest snow pit in the area; it is covered in ivy and has been partially restored. Go round this snow pit to the right and up to the **Pou del Canyo (11)**, newly renovated with a stone roof. Shortly afterwards you come to the **Casa del Canyo (12**; you could follow the track signposted 'Ibi por Camí dels Gelaors'; although shorter it runs monotonously round long drawn-out bends down the hillside). So, turn right down the broad stony track to the junction of two *barrancos*, then past a font just before the **Casa de Foiaderas (13)** and uphill again to the **crossroads (4)**.

Either turn left and return the way you came or carry straight on along the PR-CV 127, an unsurfaced roadway, which descends steeply in places to the Cruce de Venta Cuernos in the **Barranco de los Molinos (14)**. The last half hour of the walk through the *barranco* passes 3 mills, two deep caves, picnic tables and a climbing area – a delightful end to this long walk! When you reach the road turn left to the **starting point (1)**.

The Molí de la Tía Roseta, the second mill in the Barranco de los Molinos.

128

Steep walk onto a dramatic summit

The Migjorn is most easily accessible from Alicante along the N-340 towards Alcoi, but it's a beautiful, scenic drive westwards from La Torre de les Maçanes especially in February during almond blossom time. The walk ascends the easten side of Migjorn (also Mighorn) past the impressive Peña del Mediodía and descends beside the Barranco de la Cueva de los Corrales.

Location: Xixona (Jijona), 454m, on the N-340 Alicante – Alcoi, or via the CV-780 from La Torre de les Maçanes.
Starting point: Barranco de la Font, 580m. From the town centre follow signs to Tibi, past the *castillo* on the left, and just before the 2km stone turn right (sign '*solo residentes*') onto the narrow road, park at the PR-CV 212 signpost.
Height difference: 670m.
Grade: first part of the walk on gently ascending paths, then long, steep ascent all the way to the col, some sections of exposure to the summit (head for heights needed).
Maps: IGN-CNIG 846-IV/847-III.
Food/accommodation: in Xixona.
Worth seeing: 1. The Museo del Turrón shows the origins of *turrón* production, a kind of nougat, available all year round, but eaten traditionally at Christmas (www.museodelturron.com). 2. Small village of Tibi with Arab castle from 10th century and the Pantano (reservoir, southeast of the village) built in 16th century, the oldest working reservoir in Europe.

From the **PR-CV 212 signpost (1)** start the walk along the little asphalt road that leads up to a house, then continue to the right up a stony track that runs along the right hand side of a small terraced valley planted with olive trees. The path gets steeper and heads directly for the striking rock face of Peña del Mediodía past almond trees. You soon come to a signpost indicating 'Peña Mighorn, 1 hr.' in the **Barranco del Tío Pintado (2)**; turn up left here. The narrower rocky path zigzags uphill; the hillside is covered in yellow gorse in February, also rosemary, thyme and Mediterranean scrub plants. You reach a **fork (3)** 45 mins. from the start; go left here up to a broad track and left again round a house ('62 Pino y la Pineta'). Continue uphill along a track and about 2 mins. lat-

View of the Peña del Mediodía on the ascent in February at the start of the walk.

er be careful not to miss a PR-CV waymarker on a rock that indicates right along a narrow **path** (**4**; straight on brings you to a house). 25 mins. after this junction you reach a clump of pine trees; the path is now covered in loose stones and zigzags more steeply uphill. The overhanging rock face of the Peña del Mediodía towers above you on the right. Continue up along the left edge of a gorge on a scree-covered path to the head of the valley with its old stone terracing.

An exhausting incline up a wooded slope follows a level section. You finally reach a **col** (**5**; 1115m; large cairn) and enjoy breathtaking views southwards down into the gorge. Now the serious stuff begins. Look right for the yellow

The impressively overhanging Peña del Mediodía de Xixona.

and white waymarkers on the rock and climb the stepped rock, using your hands where necessary, up through a groove and down the other side. An airy traverse begins up across the rock following the best path almost on the same level as the waymarkers. A grade 1 scramble brings you to the start of a dusty path. ¼ hr. from the col you reach another col between the two summits. (A short detour to the right along a path close to the edge brings you to the summit of the Peña del Mediodia de Xixona, ¼ hr. there and back). Now follow the PR-CV 212 to the left and straight on past a signpost to reach the summit of **Peña Migjorn (6)** with a concrete pillar and a small metal box with a book for signatures.

Back at the signpost turn down left and descend the step-like rock until, a good 15 mins. later, you meet the path along the **Barranco de la Cueva de los Corrales** (**7**; sign 'Xixona 1.20 hrs.')

The path descends down the side of the *barranco* and about 20 mins. from the last signpost walk across a terraced hillside over rock slabs with the sound of choughs echoing above. You pass a small *casita* on the right. At a signpost carry straight on down the path which soon bends sharp right to descend more steeply down a narrow stony path. Cross over a track leading to a house and follow the path that leads to another **track (8)**; turn right here. In February/March the beautiful 'pink explosions' of the almond blossom are a stunning sight. You are now heading again towards the sheer Peña del Mediodía, this time from the north. Look out for a yellow and white waymarker guiding you along a narrow **path (9)** over a rise, then carry on straight across another track. Soon afterwards you meet your **ascent path (3)** which you follow back downhill to your starting **point (1)**.

View through the old stone archway in Tibi to the summit of Migjorn.

Summit ascent with a sting in the tail

This short walk goes onto the summit of the Maigmó massif which is home to extensive pine and holm oak forests. At the foot of the Maigmó lies the Tibi reservoir, 369m, which was built in 1595 to control the Verd river. The water was used for the irrigation of Alicante fruit and vegetable plantations. From the Balcón de Alicante (with picnic tables) you can enjoy extensive views of Alicante and towards the sea. An info board offers two other waymarked routes, PR-CV 238 'Riu Verd' and PR-CV 239 'Maigmó–Tibi'.

Starting point: Balcón de Alicante, 988m. On the A-7 von Alicante towards Alcoi/Castalla take the second Agost exit onto the CV-827, about 12km along the A-7 from San Vicente del Raspeig (there's a right turning to the Tibi reservoir before the Agost turn-off). Go left under the main road, round the roundabout towards Agost, shortly afterwards turn right onto the *Camí de Servei* that runs parallel to the main road. After about 2.5km turn left onto a narrow road (sign 'Parque Natural del Maigmó') and drive uphill round bends to the Balcón de Alicante; park here.
Height difference: 310m.
Grade: steep, challenging ascent on slippery, stony paths, rock scramble at the top.
Map: IGN-CNIG 846-IV.

Food: Tibi, Área de Servicio Xirau at the A-7 turn-off.
Worth seeing: 1. Tibi with castle and reservoir (see Walk 44). 2. Flea market in Castalla (15–17 May; tourist info, Plaza Mayor 3), market (Tue/Sun). 3. Ceramics on CV-820 south from Agost.
Alternative: park at the turning after 2.5km and walk up the beautiful forest road to the viewpoint (snowpit off to the left on right hairpin bend).

El Maigmó (3)
(2) 1296 m
1144 m
Balcón de ✝ (2) **Balcón de**
Alicante (I)   **Alicante (I)**
988 m   988 m
     2.2 km
0 0.55 1.30 h

The exposed summit of El Maigmó.

El Maigmó with palm trees and vines in the foreground.

From the viewing platform of the aptly named **Balcón de Alicante (1)** head uphill quite steeply through the pine forest on a stony path with natural steps over tree roots and rock. After several minutes the path gets steeper and is covered in scree. You gain height quickly and pass mountain oaks overgrown with lichen which is especially pretty in the spring. In places over smooth rock you reach a **col (2)** after about 25 mins. where a short ascent to the right directly behind the pine trees brings you to a viewpoint: Castalla in the northwest and Ibi in the northeast. The path now becomes very steep as it ascends difficult terrain. Near the top keep left, then scramble up the rock (Grade 1) to the right onto the pre-summit of **El Maigmó**. To reach the actual **summit (3)** you need to either jump over an exposed gap in the rocks, or carefully climb down across it. A wide-sweeping panorama lies at your feet. On the rock behind you there's a memorial to the mountaineer Andrés Ferrer Montalban who died on Annapurna in the Himalaya.

Return the same way to the **col (2)** where you ignore the narrow waymarked path to the left – a dangerous 2m rock step near the bottom should only be attempted by experienced mountain walkers. From the col there's a choice of path to return to the **Balcón de Alicante (1)**.

135

Peaceful walk onto a panoramic summit and to a cave

This walk is a good introduction to the extensive and beautiful recreational area of Xorret de Catí with picnic tables and barbecue sites in the heart of some stunning forest scenery. The walk leads southeastwards onto L' Alt de Guixop with beautiful views of the surrounding countryside and returns via an interesting small cave. There are several other waymarked walks of varying difficulty which begin from the hotel or a bit further southwest at the Rabosa picnic area.

Starting point: Hotel Xorret de Catí (at present closed) in the recreational area of the same name. 894m. Take the A-7 from Alicante via San Vicente del Raspeig towards Alcoi to the Castalla exit (CV-815), turn left at the second roundabout and left again at the traffic lights (brown signs 'Xorret de Catí'), just under 10km to the hotel.
Height difference: 430m.
Grade: moderate on the PR-CV 31, but with rather faint waymarkers; steep, slippery descent from the cave.
Map: IGN-CNIG 846-IV.

Food: Hotel Xorret de Catí closed until further notice; barbecue site with snackbar to the north of it.
Worth seeing: the castle (*castell*) at Castalla.
Remarks: In the Xorret de Catí area there are several waymarked easy to demanding hiking paths, such as the PR-CV 332 Pico del Fraile (from the hotel, moderate, 10km), or the PR-CV 6.6 Rabosa – Silla del Cid (from the Rabosa picnic site, south of the hotel, follow the road to Petrer, moderate to difficult, 14km).

From the back of **Hotel Xorret de Catí (1)** walk downhill to the signposts and turn diagonally left down a track (your descent route comes down the tarmac road on the left). Follow the track as it swings round to the right a few minutes later through arable fields. About 500m further on keep right at the **fork (2)**. Just after the bend before the **Mas del Carrascalet (3)** continue straight ahead (signpost) up between two waymarkers on trees. The path makes a shortcut across the bend in the track, joins it again soon after when you turn left and walk behind the house following the waymarkers. After a good 2 mins. be careful not to miss a turn up right onto a terrace **(4)**. The path narrows now as it climbs more steeply up a rocky path through the for-

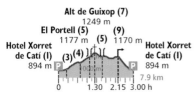

Alt de Guixop (7)
1249 m
El Portell (5)   (9)
1177 m (5) 1170 m
Hotel Xorret (3)(4)   Hotel Xorret
de Catí (I)   de Catí (I)
894 m P 1000m P 894 m
7.9 km
0   1.30 2.15 3.00 h

est until, after a good 1¼ hrs. from the start of the walk, you reach a T-junction on the col of **El Portell (5)**. Turn right along the broad drivable track and just 200m further on, right again up a narrow steep rocky **path (6)** to a signpost at the top. A few metres to the right

View across the recreational area towards the saddle-shaped Silla del Cid (Walk 48).

brings you to the summit of **Alt de Guixop** (**7**; just under 15 mins. from the col) with a 360° panorama. Return to the signpost and carry straight on downhill and at the bottom turn sharp left (straight on to the antennas; a very difficult path to El Maigmó suitable only for experienced mountain walkers) to return to the junction on the **col (5)**. Keep along the track until it descends leisurely after about 1km to a distinctive right hand bend. Take the path here which turns up to the left past a ploughed **field (8)**. A short way along turn right uphill, then a few minutes later turn left to skirt a high barren plain and

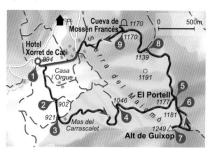

at the far end descend through trees to the **turn-off (9)** to the **Cueva de Mossén Francés**. From the cave return to the **turn-off (9)** and descend the steep, eroded path to the right. After about ½ hr. you reach the tarmac road at the bottom which brings you back to the **Hotel Xorret de Catí (1)**.

Long day's walk over the Cerro de la Cruz onto the Sierra de la Fontanella

The impressive castle at Biar dates back to the Moors and can be seen from a long way off. As you walk down from the castle to the town hall in the square you pass through the old part of Biar which is well-preserved and tastefully renovated, with many steps and fonts, but it's also a popular destination on account of its beautiful location. This peaceful walk crosses the steep hillside eastwards behind the magnificent Santuario de Nuestra Señora de Gracia and leads along the foot of the Sierra de Onil. The walk later turns northwest towards the Sierra de la Fontanella and finally returns to Biar along a lovely undulating forest path across wooded hillsides.

Location: Biar, 700m.

Starting point: Área recreativa del Santuario de Nuestra Señora de Gracia, 770m. Follow signs from Biar towards Castalla, before the roundabout turn left at the sign 'Pou de la Neu', then go right at the T-junction past the snow pit (iron railings), continue along the road behind the Santuario (church) and then turn up right. Or from Castalla drive northwestwards on the CV-80, take the CV-799 exit towards Biar, turn right just after the 9km stone and park at the picnic and barbecue site (walking info boards).

Height difference: 600m.

Grade: many ascents and descents, mostly broad forest paths and tracks, but long steep ascent on rocky path at the start; waymarked throughout (PR-CV 55).

Maps: IGN-CNIG 820-III/846-I/II.

Food/accommodation: Hotel Rural Mas Fontanelles on the road to Banyeres.

Worth seeing: Biar is an important centre for ceramics. Worth seeing are the castle, the Iglesia de la Asunción in the square (renaissance façade, Baroque sacristy), the Pou de la Neu (snow pit), as well as the fiesta for the patron saint in May with its curious Moorish figure, the Mahoma. Info: www.biar.es.

Alternative: short walk along a rough track through open forest and down a *barranco*: shortly after Font del Soriano turn left at the fork (3) and after about ½ hr. turn left again, eventually meeting a tarmac road; go left here along the main route to Biar; 3 hrs. in total.

From the picnic area at the **Santuario de Nuestra Señora de Gracia (1)** follow the waymarkers up the steep rocky path, quickly gaining height and with wonderful views back downhill of the village and the castle. The path widens into a track and ascends steeply to a junction. Continue straight on along the narrow path lined with esparto grass, rosemary, thyme and low pine trees which leads under a power line and up ahead you can now see the antennae on the top of Reconco (1210m). The path ascends quite steeply again and about 1 hr. from the start of the walk you come to a water tank on a **col (2)** and a surfaced roadway coming up from the right from the Coll de Biar. Turn left and walk past *fincas* and beautifully cultivated almond groves to a small clump of poplars and a spring, **Font del Soriano** (info board). At the **fork (3)** just 300m further on go right (left, see Alternative), then turn right again at the

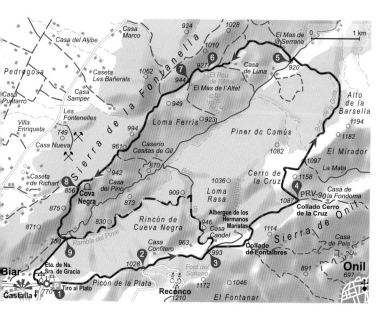

next fork past a red iron barrier along a forest track. Continue left at the following junction and pass the Albergue de los Hermanos Maristas (religious Order) on your left. At a **signpost (4)** where the PR-CV 90 turns right to Onil keep straight on. You soon come to a water tank. Ascend steeply round it on the left up the forest path at the foot of Cerro de la Cruz. The path leads downhill again and at a conspicuous left hand bend you can just about make out the remains of a small snow pit on the left, now covered in moss and vegetation. Descend the bumpy forest track and pass another barrier. Now walk across an open stretch of land to a roadway; turn left here (PR-CV 35 goes right to Banyeres).

The roadway goes straight on to Biar in just under 8km, but you turn to the right instead **(5)** and follow the now narrower track through the forest. Ignore

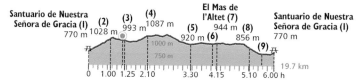

El Pou de l'Altet, an old well at the side of the path.

all turnings to the right and left and look out carefully for waymarkers. The path widens and you pass a large white *finca* (El Mas de la Serrana). About 2km further on you come past an old stone well, **El Pou de l'Altet (6)**, and shortly after that **El Mas de l'Altet** on your left on a hill. Turn right here along a track **(7)**.

At the following fork go right and eventually under a power line. The path gets much narrower and stonier and leads down past a left hand turn-off to the **Cova Negra (8)**. A few minutes later, if you look back left, you can see the cave high up in the rock. You arrive at another fork in the path; turn down to the tarmac road (**9**; the short walk joins here from the left). Turn right towards Biar and pass the entrance to the Lomas de Java camping and barbecue site, no longer open. As you approach the village follow the tarmac road uphill on the left. At a fork ignore the yellow and white waymarker on a tree indicating right (down into the town of Biar) and continue uphill to the left in a few minutes back to the **Santuario (1)**.

The impressive castle of Biar dominates the countryside.

Alto de la Silla del Cid, 1152m

Walk onto an imposing massif

The northern summit of the Sierra del Cid is called the 'saddle of El Cid' and rises up above the Medio Vinalopó. El Cid is the name by which Rodrigo Díaz de Vivar, the Spanish national hero, was known at the time of the Reconquista. This impressive massif is a landmark for the towns in the area, Novelda, Elda, Petrer, Monforte del Cid and Agost, and its distinctive table mountain shape can be seen for miles around. Its topography and accessibility have made it a popular area for climbers and mountain walkers, while the southern summit of the Sierra del Cid is a favourite with mountain bikers.

Location: Petrer, 461m.
Starting point: junction below El Cid, 630m. From the A-31 motorway Alicante – Madrid take the Petrer (norte)/Centro Comercial exit, then drive towards Xorret de Catí, turn right shortly after the 1km stone (sign 'Vía Pecuària') very steeply downhill, cross a ford and keep left at the top of the road. Go straight over two roundabouts and follow the road at first parallel to the motorway, then round to the left uphill past the 'Área recreativa Villa Ferrusa'. At the top park near the PR-CV 36 sign.
Height difference: 540m.
Grade: steady ascent on a zigzag path to the ridge, mostly in the shade; yellow and white PR-CV waymarkers. Last 3.5km of the walk on tarmac.
Map: IGN-CNIG 871-I.
Food/accommodation: in Petrer.
Worth seeing: Petrer.
Alternative: 10 mins. after the summit go right along the broad path which narrows after about 5 mins., ascend the hillside, cross over a *barranco* and reach a cross path; go straight over and then downhill until you meet your ascent path (3); turn left here (about 1 hr. shorter in total).
Tip: lovely recreational area at Xorret de Catí northeast of Petrer with picnic and barbecue site (see Walk 46).

From the **signpost (1)** waymarked 'PR-CV 36 Cumbre del Cid' turn right up the path steeply at first and parallel to the roadway. The path broadens out briefly, then continues round an old terrace. It's a long steep ascent up a zigzag path and you quickly gain height (ignore all shortcuts); the path continues up the wooded hillside and leads across a scree slope. Just under 1 hr. from the start you reach a **col (2)** with a viewpoint from where you can see the sea and the Sierra del Cid as it bends round to the south. Now ascend the rock slabs and come to another ridge where you meet a broader **path (3)**. Walk along this path to the left (right, see Alternative) and finally ascend loose scree up the main broad ridge of the mountain to an enormous cairn on the summit of **Alto de la Silla del Cid (4)**.

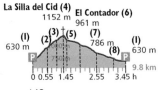

142

A striking, chunky mountain – Alto de la Silla del Cid.

Views extend to the Maigmó in the northeast and further on to the Migjorn. From the summit walk down through some bushes and descend a short easy section of rock (waymarker) onto a steep, slippery path. About 10 mins. down this zigzag path brings you to a broader path where you turn left (**5**; the shorter walk goes right here, see Alternative). About 45 mins. from the summit, after two gentle ascents, you come steeply down to a col, **El Contador**. At the point where the path begins to ascend once more, the PR-CV 6.6 turns off left. Leave the main path which continues southwards along the Sierra del Cid and turn right at the cairns into the wood (**6**). Descend the forest path to a shallow gully and follow it round to the left. A few minutes later the path leads to the right towards some orange-coloured crags and then zigzags steeply downhill below the overhanging rocks. Continue downhill to reach a narrow **tarmac road (7)** which you follow to the right. Walk for about 3.5km down the road with lovely views of the Sierra and past the Pouet del Pi de l'Aire. Shortly afterwards you can take a path to the right **(8)** to shorten one of the bends and return in a good 15 mins. to your **starting point (1)**.

A walk along St James' Way, a 'gingerbread' church and a summit

This walk brings you from the town of Novelda situated on the Río Vinalopó along beside the fast flowing river even in summer, uphill via the sanctuary of María Magdalena and the castle onto the summit of La Mola. Novelda is famous for its marble industry, the cultivation of saffron (Sp. azafran), the table grapes that are grown in paper bags, and its Art Nouveau buildings (Sp. modernismo), of which the sanctuary of María Magdalena is one. The walk also follows a short section of the St James Way from Alicante to Santiago de Compostela (Camino de Santiago del Sureste).

Starting point: northern edge of Novelda, 257m. From the N-330 via the CV-820 into town, follow the pink signs for the 'Santuario' (or 'Castillo de la Mola') and just before the bridge over the Río Vinalopó turn left and then right to the tree-lined Plaza de la Magdalena. Turn immediately right along the CV-832, past the Diputación de Alicante, as far as a PR-CV 311 signpost to the Castillo on the right (just before the 1km stone); park at the side of the road.

Height difference: 320m.

Grade: easy walk on yellow and white marked tracks and paths (PR-CV 311), waymarked almost throughout, short scramble near the summit; no shade except at the Santuario.

Map: IGN-CNIG 871-III.

Food/accommodation: in Novelda; café at the Santuario.

Worth seeing: 1. In the town centre Centro Cultural 'Gómez-Tortosa' (tourist office (Oficina de Turismo), open Tues–Fri 10–14.00, 16–18.30, Mon, Sat 10–14.00), many Art Nouveau buildings (e.g. Casa Museo Modernista), the Iglesia de San Pedro (1553), the Casino. 2. Just under 3km north of the town the castle (12th century) with tri-angular tower, and the Santuario de Santa María Magdalena (Art Nouveau building designed by D. José Sala Sala, built 1918–46; two slim cylindrical bell towers, inside the works of A. Castellano and Gastón Castelló with scenes from the life of María Magdalena). 3. The Parque del Oeste on the CV-835 towards Monóvar. 4. Wine cellars (*bodegas*), in Novelda (e.g. Heretat de Cesilia, restaurant and winery, www.heretatdecesilia.com), Monóvar and Pinoso. Further info: www.novelda.es.

Alternative: for a shorter walk, drive to the Castillo/Santuario car park (road ends here), walk up to the summit of La Mola, then return to the castle (see end of description; a good 1¾ hr.).

Tip: the best time to undertake this walk is at the weekend when the noise from the motorway on the other side of the valley is less obtrusive.

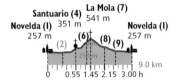

Follow the **signposts (1)** for the PR-CV 311 and the Camino de Santiago del Sureste to the right. The broad track soon becomes a tarmac roadway which then meets a broader road where you carry straight on next to the Visemar

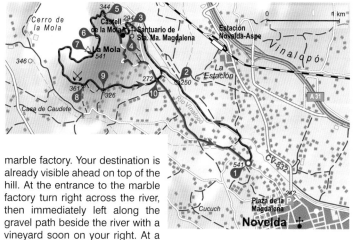

marble factory. Your destination is already visible ahead on top of the hill. At the entrance to the marble factory turn right across the river, then immediately left along the gravel path beside the river with a vineyard soon on your right. At a fork go left and cross the **Río Vinalopó (2)** on large blocks of pink and white marble used as stepping stones. Eventually you arrive at the SER y ACA marble factory. Turn left up the tarmac road, then right up the road that comes down from the castle past a chimney that belonged to the Magdalena electricity company from 1898. After 150m you come to a **PR-CV sign-post (3)** on your left with an interpretative sign for El Partidor del Castell. Climb left up the steep rocky path; a slippery section is made safe with a

The Castillo (left) and Santuario as seen below from the the Río Vinalopó.

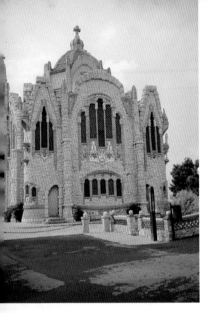

The beautiful Art Nouveau building of the Santuario de Santa María Magdelena.

handrail. You quickly reach the **Santuario de Santa María Magdalena (4**; benches in the shade, café and toilets). The church is constructed mainly of marble and small river stones. It's worth taking a look inside the church where, contrary to its elaborate exterior, the inside appears rather plain (May–Sept. 10–14.00 and 17–20.00, Oct.–Apr. 10–14.00 and 16–19.00, changes possible).

Turn right and walk round La Mola castle of Almohade origin and constructed on the site of an ancient Roman fortress. At the car park turn right downhill, then left at the far end up a broad initially concrete track past a small abandoned quarry and at a **PR-CV signpost (5)** ascend left up a rocky path. As you quickly gain height be careful not to miss the **waymarker (6)** guiding you left up to the ridge. Continue up the crest of the ridge from where there are distant views of the surrounding mountains such as La Silla del Cid (see Walk 48; half way up an info board with names). At the next signpost turn right up a rough and loose rocky path in 5 mins. to the summit of **La Mola (7)**. Back at the signpost turn right down the broad track. Just under ½ hr. from the summit you come past a stone shepherds´ shelter and **corral (8)** off to the left and a few paces afterwards turn left uphill, then immediately left again. Be careful here – after about 50m the route swings right (due to erosion, possibly no waymarker) and 5 mins. later you meet a **tarmac road (9)**. Turn left down the road and about 10 mins. after that you meet the **main road (10)**; turn right to reach your **starting point (1)** in about 20 mins.

Alternative: to avoid the tarmac road walk straight across the **main road (10)** and down to the path beside the river; turn right here in 20 mins. to the car. Or, for the shorter Alternative, walk left back up the road to the castle approach road, turn left here, then immediately right up a narrow roadway and beautifully constructed steps to the castle area. If you haven't parked here, follow the same path back to Novelda.

On the way from the castle to the summit of La Mola.

A jewel in the Mediterranean

1800m long and at the broadest point a maximum width of 450m, the flat island of Tabarca lies 11 sea miles away from Alicante as the continuation of the Cabo de Santa Pola. Carlos III had the island fortified in 1760 to drive away the Barbary pirates who had used it earlier as a place of refuge. He repopulated the island with 600 Genoese fishermen who had been taken prisoner by Africans in the Tunisian harbour of Tabarka – which later gave the island its name. The king bought their freedom on 8 December 1768 and sent them with their families to the island which was called at that time Isla Plana or Planesia (plano means flat). The Italian names of many of its inhabitants today (Parodi, Ruso, Chacopino) are evidence of its past history. Tabarca is a borough of Alicante and the only inhabited island in the Valencian community. The absence of cars, the wonderful coves and the many fish specialities make Tabarca a wonderful place for a day trip. The island and the waters around it were listed as a marine reserve in 1986, the first in Spain, due to their important ecosystems.

Starting point: the quay in the small harbour of Tabarca. Boats to Tabarca leave from Torrevieja, Guardamar, Alicante and Benidorm, although for the most frequent crossings, widest choice of boats and shortest journey of about half an hour, it is best to depart from Santa Pola (timetable: www.islatabarca.com or www.alicante-turismo.com).

Height difference: insignificant.

Grade: easy walk on broad paths and village roads.

Maps: IGN-CNIG 894-III/914B-I.

Food/accommodation: a good choice of restaurants; recommended Restaurant Gloria with good views, Hotel Boutique Isla Tabarca (former governor's residence), friendly service from José Navarro, the manager; www.alicanteturismo.com.

Worth seeing: 1. The small museum opposite the harbour (exhibition of history, geology and sea life, closed Mon).
2. The old entrance gates.
3. The Governor's house, restored and now a hotel.
4. The church of San Pedro y San Pablo which was completed in 1779.

Tip: take water shoes and swimwear with you. Snorkel equipment can be bought on the island.

From the quay at the **harbour** of **Tabarca** (**1**; make a note of the return boat times) go up the steps on the left to the large sundial and past some restaurants (beach over to the right). Follow a broad sandy path which leads you around the right hand side of the eastern half of the island. On the right you will soon see a shrine built into the rocks and several narrow paths go down steeply to small rocky coves. Continue past the restored **Torre de San José** (**2**; built in 1790) and a few minutes later pass the lighthouse surrounded by a tall wire fence which today houses a biological laboratory.

The old gateway into the walled town of Tabarca.

At the end of the fence keep right. Apart from some large solitary hedgehog cactus plants in the middle of the island the island is quite barren, for which you are now more than compensated by the wonderful views out to sea. You are now heading towards the walls of the **cemetery (3)**. Go past it on the right hand side to reach the furthermost point of the island. In August we saw a swarm of kimbrels, a turnstone, a single swallow, herring gulls and common terns. This end of the island is especially popular with snorkellers. Return along the other side of the island where there are more small rocky bays to explore. Once you have arrived back at the **harbour (1)**, carry straight on past the restaurants and beach and through the main gateway. The walled town was declared a historical national monument in 1964 and is an interesting example of the concept of a fortified town in the 18th century.

The pretty main street leads directly to the other end of the island, but turn right after the gateway, left, then right before Hostal Nueva Masín and left again towards a **second gateway (4)**. Turn immediately left through a short tunnel and then right to cross the square past the church (renovated in 2004; alternatively turn right up the steps past the church to walk along the town walls) and straight on to a **third gateway (5)** at the western end of the island. A sign warns you of this dangerous slippery area.

Back at the **gateway (5)** continue right (south), past Plaça Gran with the very reasonably priced Restaurant Casa Ramos to a small rocky bay with crystal clear water. Shortly afterwards turn right past another bay to continue along the town walls (on your left the old **Casa del Gobernador**; 6) and past Restaurante Gloria back to the main beach in a wide-sweeping bay with shallow waters. Walk up left past the beach and back to the **harbour (1)**.

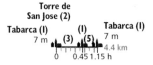

View from the island of Tabarca of the Cabo de Santa Pola on the mainland.

Airy walk full of surprises

The mountain range of the Sierra de Orihuela lies north of the town of the same name and extends westwards into the neighbouring region of Murcia. It is made up of limestone and Dolomitic rock with very steep walls and many rock crevices. This varied walk follows an adventurous route up from the south to the Cruz de la Muela, then leads rather airily across the steeply sloping hillside before climbing onto the Peña de Orihuela from where you can see as far as the Sierra de Cartagena and the Mar Menor in the region of Murcia.

Starting point: Barranco de Bonanza, 80m, north of Orihuela: drive westwards on the N-340 to the 685km stone (bar/restaurant El Piste on the left, closed), take the second turning right (signpost 'PR CV-59 III, Senda de San Cristóbal'; not the first one which is also signposted) for just under 1km to the sign 'Pinar de Bonanza'; park at the left hand bend.

Height difference: 875m.

Grade: moderate to difficult walk, exposed sections above the Paso del Gato (cat's pass), lengthy, steep descent; PR CV 59 waymarkers.

Map: IGN-CNIG 913-II.

Food/accommodation: in Orihuela.

Worth seeing: 1. Orihuela with its beautiful buildings (Gothic, Renaissance, Baroque; leaflets available from the town hall), especially the Gothic Iglesia de las Santas Justa y Rufina. Info: www.orihuelaturistica.es (also in English) and www.orihuela.es. 2. About ½ hr. southeast of Orihuela, Las Lagunas de la Mata y Torrevieja Natural Park (information office opposite Torrelamata on the N-332 north of Torrevieja; lovely circular walk around the lake, particularly interesting for birdwatchers, the lagoons provide nesting places and winter quarters for more than 100 species of aquatic birds; together with the natural parks of El Hondo and Salinas de Santa Pola the salt flats of Torrevieja are a wetlands area of great international importanc; the salt is exported all over the world). 3. The salt flats of Santa Pola with its resident population of flamingos.

Alternative: 'black' walk via the Paso del Gato to the high mountain path (about 1 hr. shorter): exposed with a bit of scrambling needed.

Remarks: little shade on this walk, don't forget sun protection and plenty of water.

From the left hand follow the rough track northwards and at the fork turn left into the forest to a **cross path (1)**. Turn right (your descent route joins here from the left) and follow the path for about 10 mins. to a derelict building, the **Casa Forestal (2**; former forestry house), and then turn left uphill looking out for waymarkers. It's a steep ascent now over colourful layers of minerals in the rock as you head towards three caves. About half an hour from the start a sign painted on the rock guides you left to the **Paso del Gato (3**; see Alternative), but continue right up a broken ramp with some exposure, but with good footholds, then less steeply uphill. After another ½ hr. you reach the **col (4)**. Continue right along the almost level path to the foot of the **Cruz de**

The town of Orihuela sits below a backdrop of mountains.

la Muela and after a short ascent, you reach the **summit (5)** with views of the Sierra de Callosa opposite (the PR-CV 54 leads there). Back at the signpost on the **col (4)** descend to the right along a rocky but level path, this time on the northern side of the ridge. Some minutes later, after a waymarked turn-off right down the Senda de las Minas, descend steeply to the left through a **rocky gap (6)**. The now beautiful high mountain path on the southern side of the ridge leads below an orange-coloured sculpted rock face with slightly exposed sections in places. Feathery bushes of esparto grass line the path in spring. About 40 mins. from the col you meet the junction with the path leading down to the **Paso del Gato (7;** see Alternative). Continue along to the right here on an undulating path in the direction of the Peña de Orihuela (sign '1 hr. 35 mins.') and Raiguero Levante (sign '3 hrs.'). At a **fork (8)** the path swings round to the left and begins to ascend once more. Keep a look-out for the next waymarkers on the rock slabs across the vegetated sloping hillside which guide you up to the top left hand edge. Ascend a steep rocky path and continue up the rise to a skyline tree before reaching the meadow bowl of La Naveta, an ideal **spot for a picnic (9)**.

From here to the summit of **Peña de Orihuela**: climb the

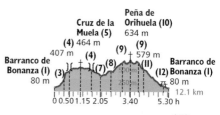

153

rock wall diagonally right. The path contours up and down round two hills before reaching the **summit (10)**, with a bit of scrambling, in 25 mins.

Back at the **turn-off (9)** turn steeply down a stony path on the right to a fork; turn left here towards San Cristóbal **(11)**. Then follows an extraordinary landscape of rust-red and slate-blue mineral-stained rocks that contrast with the bright green pines. Later on descend a large area of rock fall. It's a long slippery descent of almost an hour, at one point along a severely eroded path where there's a cable for protection, until you eventually reach the picnic area of **El Pinar de Bonanza (12)**. Turn right and then left, round the cabins, to follow the broad forest track northeastwards downhill to the **cross-roads (1)**; turn right to the car.

Below: at the Paso del Gato.
Right: view back from the ramp of the prohibited climbing area due to conservation.

Index

Castilian	Valencian	English
abajo	avall, abaix	bewol
acampada	acampada	place to camp (free)
águila	àguila	eagle
agujero	forat	hole
alto	alt	hill, high
apartamento	apartament	apartment
área recreativa	àrea recreativa	picnic area
arriba	dalt	above
ayuntamiento	ajuntament	town hall
bajo	baix	low
bancal	bancal	terrace
barranco	barranc	gorge, ravine
bodega	bodega	wine cellar
calle	carrer	street
camino	camí	track, path
campo	camp	countryside
carretera	carretera	road
casa rural	casa rural	small country B&B
castillo	castell	castle
castellano	castellà	Castilian
caza	caça	huntin
cerro, colina	puig, tossal	hill
collado	coll	pass, col
coto de caza	coto de caça	hunting ground
cueva	cova	cave
cucummbre	cim	summit
depósito de agua	dipòsit d'aigua	water tank
embalse	embassament	reservoir
era	era	threshing place
ermita	ermita	hermitage
faro	far	lighthouse
ferrocarril	ferrocarril	railway
finca	finca	(country) property
folleto	fullet	Prospekt
fuente	font	leaflet
hostal	hostal	cheap hotel
hoyo	clot	hole, pit
huerta	horta	allotment
inglés	angles	English
lavadero	llavador	wash house
loma	lloma, tossal	hill, ridge
mapa	mapa	map
masía/mas	masia/mas	farmstead, manor house
mirador	mirador	viewpoint
monte/montaña	mont/muntaya	mountain
nevera	nevera	snow pit

peligroso	perillós	dangerous
peña	penya	rock, cliff
peñón	penyó	rock, cliff
pensión	pensió	B&B
pista forestal	pista forestal	forest track
plaza	plaça	square
pozo (de nieve)	pou (de neu)	snow pit
puente	pont	bridge
puerto	port	harbour
rcfugio	refugi	mountain hut
río	riu	river
roca	roca	rock
sendero/senda	sender/senda	path, footpath
sierra	serra	mountain range
sima	alvenc/avenc	fissures
torre	torre	tower
valenciano	valencià	Valencian
valle	vall	valley
via pecuària	via pecuari	cattle track

Cover photo: a well-known landmark on the Costa Blanca, the Peñón de Ifach (Walk 16), as seen from the Sierra de Oltà (Walk 15).

Frontispiece: view from the Sierra de Oltà (Walk 15) of the Sierra Helada (Walks 18 and 19).

Phote page24/25: Benifato castle (Walk 29).

All photos by Gill Round and Terry Gifford except for those on pages 65 and 69 by Cordula Rabe.

Kartografie:
51 small walking maps to a scale of 1:50,000 and 1:75,000
© Bergverlag Rother GmbH, Munich
(drawn by Barbara Häring, Gröbenzell)

Two overview maps to a scale of 1:700,000 and 1:1.500,000
© Freytag & Berndt, Vienna

All the walks described in this guide are accurate to the best knowledge of the author. The use of this guide is at one's own risk. The publishers accept no legal responsibility for accidents or injuries of any kind.

2nd, completely revised edition 2014
© Bergverlag Rother GmbH, Munich

ISBN 978-3-7633-4837-4

We look forward to any suggestions for improvements to this walking guide!
BERGVERLAG ROTHER · Munich
D-82041 Oberhaching · Keltenring 17 · Tel. +49 89 608669-0
Internet www.rother.de · E-Mail leserzuschrift@rother.de